Casual Talk
on
Philosophy, Religion
and
Good Life

MAKMOR TUMIN

Published by:

Unit No. E-10-5, Jalan SS 15/4G, Subang Square,
47500 Subang Jaya, Selangor, Malaysia
+603-7772-3156 (office) / +6017-399-7411 (mobile)
info@tertib.press
www.tertib.press
@tertibpress (Facebook & Instagram)

Author	:	Makmor Tumin
Editor	:	Norashikin Azizan
Cover designer	:	Rasydan Mahzan
Typesetter	:	Abdul Adzim Md Daim

CASUAL TALK ON PHILOSOPHY, RELIGION, AND GOOD LIFE

First Edition: May 2022

Perpustakaan Negara Malaysia   Cataloguing-in-Publication Data

Makmor Tumin
Casual Talk on Philosophy, Religion and Good Life / Makmor Tumin.
ISBN 978-967-2844-10-5
1. Makmor Tumin--Anecdotes.
2. Philosophy.
3. Religion.
4. Conduct of life.
I. Title.
100

Contents

Preface

Are there any basic requirements for you to read this book? Curiosity is all that is required for you to read and understand this book.

This is not an academic book. I targeted it for the public or for those who have just joined the ivory tower. Anyone of any belief or religion can follow along the ideas that are presented in this book. It is an extension of my lecture notes, drawn from the course *GBE0018: Philosophy, Religion, and Spiritual Life*. This book is presented in a style which I prefer to call conversationalism, with some dose of my own stories or fashionably known as personal anecdotes, motivated by a set of philosophical questions fostered to me by my friends who were at a certain point studying at the institution where I teach (University of Malaya). If there are arguments or theses to be made, they are: We can only advance our knowledge of philosophy and religion if we have the strong curiosity to know, and one way to know is through asking questions. I do not think that this sort of curiosity would kill the cat.

Questions that are asked out of ego, hatred, or anger will not make you any more knowledgeable. Even at worst, it only invites other people's ego, hatred, and anger. As you are reading this book, I should perhaps give you the gist of the contents of this book. The *Introduction* or *Chapter 1* contains my responses to three philosophical questions that I retrieved from my friends. *Chapter 2* details the importance of curiosity and humility in pursuing knowledge of philosophy and religion. *Chapter 3* talks about the primary things people learn when they study philosophy and religion. *Chapter 4* explains the reason for us to try to learn and understand more about philosophy. *Chapter 5* provides an extended discussion on the importance of religion. *Chapter 6* is basically a tour of the many religions of the world. *Chapter 7* is a discussion of the Unseen World or the metaphysics. *Chapter 8* highlights the main ideas or laws that govern existence of the world. *Chapter 9* discusses the question of evil and radical individual choice. Finally, the *Conclusion* or *Chapter 10* explores the idea of philosophy in Islam.

While my basic knowledge on moral and political philosophy was generally introduced to me by Ian Shapiro, Michael Sandel, and Steven Smith's works, my knowledge of Islam highly depends on Timothy Winter, Yasir Qadhi, and Mark Hanson's works. I don't think this book could have materialised into its current form without my engagement with their works, especially those uploaded on YouTube.

The contents of this book are organised in questions to give you a dialogue-like experience, or to be exact a Q&A session, a method which people should apply to better pursue their knowledge. I must thank those who helped me with the materialisation of this book. The list is too long. Teamwork definitely made this dream work. Suffice for me to say thanks to all my family members and three of my friends and colleagues, as well as a student whose participation in class is very memorable and admirable to me.

I can be contacted through my email makmor.tumin@gmail.com. Some of my other works can be found on my website godconsciousness.info, of which you can visit to know more about me and my works.

CHAPTER 1

Introduction:
Philosophy or
Religiophilosophy
Clinic?

Clinics for medical questions or religious questions are available online, but this is not necessarily the case for philosophical and religiophilosophical questions. To be sure, different societies may develop their own unique philosophical questions and therefore any idea of clinics for philosophical questions must cater for the needs of their society. If you say no, we do not need a clinic, you should at least read till the end of this chapter, as it may just flip a switch and change your mind. If you do change your mind and believe that yes, we do need such a clinic, there is a good reason for you to continue reading the following chapters of this book.

This chapter is based on email interviews with former students of Universiti Malaya who during their studies, demonstrated their keen interest on philosophical questions. Answers for the questions are based on three respondents, and all of the philosophical questions came from them, be it from their heart or questions collected from their readings or discussions with their friends.

Responses to Questions from Respondent 1

1. *Why do we need religion to define morality?*

This is a good question. We are both finite and infinite

beings. Our body is finite, which means it will be destroyed. However, our soul will not perish since it is infinite or eternal. Our minds cannot comprehend absolute morality, but our soul can. Therefore, we need religion to define morality.

2. *Is morality fixed or relative?*

Morality that is based on the mind is worldly in nature, therefore relative. Activities that take place in Papua New Guinea influence the mind of the people there, and activities that influence people's minds in Las Vegas are different from the ones in Papua New Guinea. Morality that is absolute is morality that is based on activities on the infinite level.

3. *What is freedom? Is true freedom possible?*

Freedom is the ability for us to get rid of ourselves from our mind and bodily activities. Yes, true freedom is possible, and it is timeless and spaceless. It is in our infinite being through our soul.

4. *What is the meaning of life?*

We are in this world not just for the preservation of life, but also for the salvation of the soul. This is the main purpose of life. Philosophers only disagree on what is the purpose of life. Some believe that the purpose already exists in nature, while others argue that the purpose can be comprehended through our reason. It is not just for the greed of the market, but for the grace of the cathedral, as Charles Taylor said, or in my case, the grace of the mosque (the grace of the divine).

5. *What happens to a person after they die?*

Their body and mind die, but their souls do not, since they are infinite. There are many ways to explain this phenomenon. Some use karmic law and others follow the Afterlife's principles of justice. However, for those who subscribe to atheism, humans live only once, and we are here by random process. Hence, no such thing can be comprehended as an Afterlife for this group.

6. *What is love?*

True love is the love between your soul and mind. It is internal, and is the love of God. Another form of love is animalism, which happens among animals and human beings. While the former form of love infinitely flows, the latter is temporal.

7. *How do you know what is real?*

Everything is relative to our own experience which develops either from our family, genetics/gender, countries, cultures, ethnicities, and many other things.

The real thing is beyond all of these matters. It has no identity. It is about the soul and is only comprehensible through the inner process or commonly understood as religion, remembrance of God, or meditation. However, we cannot negate the immediate reality which is part of our body and mind—the finite.

8. *Is it always wrong to lie?*

It is not about what we do, but our intention. If we do not want others to lie to us, the best advice is not to lie to others. However, it is not just about the intention, but also the consequences. If we do not want terrible consequences to happen to us, it is advised not to allow bad things to happen to others as well.

9. *Why do we dream?*

I heard it is part of our amygdala process as mentioned by Michio Kaku. Dreams are activities that are real at that level but have no meaning when we wake up from it.

10. *Does fate exist?*

It works on two levels. The primary cause dictates everything, but it does not mean that the secondary cause does not operate. For example, we are, by fate, auto-cruised beings. However, this does not mean that we cannot steer right or left.

Responses to Questions from Respondent 2

1. ***What is the purpose of our individual lives? Is it a dedication to ourselves, a service to others, a worship to the Almighty, or it has no meaning, merely an inconsequential existence?*** *(My answers tend to differ based on my mood for the week, but I am inclined to think it is an over-inflated existence, we exist for no poignant "grand purpose" but it doesn't mean we should stop dedicating this life for ourselves, providing service to others, prostrating to the Almighty).*

   We are two beings, finite and infinite. The former is our body and mind, while the latter is our soul. The body and mind are subjected to activities around us, and as we die, they die, too. The latter is eternal and continues to exist even when our finite being dies. Hence, we have the purpose in this life to aim for the happiness of both our finite and infinite beings.

2. ***Do we truly have free-will? Is everything in life set in stone (Qadha' & Qadr) and to what extent do we have the freedom to choose? Do our choices then branch off to more free-will or is there a predestined path based on our earlier choice?***

Our choices are the function of our previous choices, or influenced by those previous choices, including our parents' and grandparents' choices. It also implies that when women choose to buy make ups, it is their gender which influences their choice, not necessarily free choice. The fact that we human beings didn't choose ourselves to be human, and that there is no way to choose to become monkeys or plants, implies that there is a grand choice governing us. In a nutshell, there is a primary law that causes worldly events, but it doesn't mean that a secondary law doesn't operate. We are, by nature, auto-cruise beings, already naturally set towards a specific direction, but it doesn't mean that we can't turn right or left. We are responsible for those decisions to turn right or left.

3. ***Is morality set in stone or does it move with the zeitgeist of time? What we deemed immoral three hundred years ago is perhaps moral or even expected of in the present. If so, what determines morality and if morality is constantly changing—what is true morality then? Can morality be fluid?***

All worldly morality based on the power of the human mind is subjective or fluid as you rightly said. This is so because the mind is a projection of our finite being.

Absolute morality does exist, and works for our infinite being (soul), beyond the mind. It is not based on arguments, but on our own inner experience.

4. ***Do humans owe our existence to a purpose and betterment i.e.: do we absolutely have to continue to be better people? Is it 'right' if we decide we are content with ourselves despite not achieving our best?***

The golden mean we should aim for is the middle path. Every move we take, there is always consideration for left and right, but there is a target that is naturally set for us.

5. ***Are there absolute truths or merely what we perceive as the truth? If so, then what determines truths against untruths?***

Men comprised two beings—the finite and infinite. All truths which are the projection of the mind are worldly truths and are subjective. They work at the human finite level. Only through infinite/soul-level activities, absolute truths will reveal themselves.

6. ***Do humans have souls? If medical advancement has reached a point where each inch of the human body has been cut open and scrutinised***

yet there is no definite proof that humans have a soul, then does a soul exist? And if a soul does not exist, what gives humans consciousness and individual uniqueness? To what do we owe our humanity to if not to our souls?

Fantastic question. There is no soul in the human finite being (physical body and mind), therefore medical advancements cannot discover the soul. But we are also infinite beings where the soul is located, and it is eternal (not to get confused by the finite and infinite beings understood by the Greek thinkers, in case you decide to search further on the Internet).

7. *My absolute favourite: If humanity was stuck in The Matrix, should we all choose to stay in the simulation or break free, given that the real world is bleak with nothing to live for? Is it wrong to choose to stay in the simulated illusion and just be happy? Are we being fair to ourselves for doing that?*

Your question here relates to the Experience Machine/ Pleasure Machine thought experiment introduced by Robert Nozick. If we are just finite beings, probably it is fine to just stay in the matrix—but we are not. The infinite part of us is more wondrous (colourful, beautiful, pleasurable, and can only be known by those who are experiencing it) than the pleasure machine. Thus, you have other choices which are more superior.

Responses to Questions from Respondent 3

1. ***How do we know what is the universal physical truth? Is reality simply an interpretation of the senses? E.g., Is the purple I see the same as the purple others are seeing? Does sweet taste the same for everyone? Does sound happen if no ears are present to hear it?***

Universal physical truth is known through the laws of physics, biology, and chemistry. These laws apply only in this sphere called earth, meaning that the law of gravity is different in this sphere compared to outer space. All worldly realities are interpretation of the senses. That said, our senses are still limited to worldly truth. What do we see immediately in front of us? Our standard answer would be the material we are reading. Actually, between our eyes and the material we are reading, there are many different things, excluding even air, such as millions of atoms and tachyons that are not visible to our naked eyes, not to mention other things those who have developed their inner eyes see. There is a general law that governs our sense of sight, taste, and hearing. For example, we can confirm that the falling tree does create a sound, since the law of physics states that such an impact would release energy in the form of vibrations of high amplitude, hence creating sound. One hundred identical machines can capture the same sound exactly. The same goes when it comes to the question of sight and taste. Since there are no one hundred identical humans, we all perceive things according to our unique abilities/disabilities.

2. ***If babies are considered innocent, when do people cease to be innocent? Why is it the moment we can evaluate and make decisions consciously, we are suddenly flawed beings?***

There are many ways to respond to this question. One of them is that we cease to be innocent when we are able to make conscious decisions to differentiate between what is morally good and bad, determined by different methods of maturity; biological, cultural, religious, mental, and the like. We have been "programmed" to reach a certain target/destination, and once we have matured, we are able to make conscious decisions to make detours and choose different paths to reach that target. Hence, we are flawed beings if we choose to detour from the middle/straight path which leads to the target. We are autocruise beings, but that does not mean we are unable to turn left and right.

3. ***If fate is written for every individual, are we morally obligated to help others? What if they are fated to suffer and struggle in this world?***

I hope that this is a philosophical, not a religious-specific question (I would be glad if religious questions are directed to religious experts). There are two laws that operate in this world. Layers of the first law dictates our fate. For example, "some people are born rich, and some people are born poor". The second law informs us that our role is just to help others, not to try and change their fate (helping others does not entail changing their fate in this world). Richness and poorness do not determine individual happiness and suffering, and worldly sufferings have no significance in the Other World, in which the first law or primary cause operates.

4. ***How is it fair that you are put on this world without your consent? Why is creating a human life justified but taking one's life is not?***

The philosophy of consent was popularised by the Contractarianism school of thought which believed on the idea that authority is justified through consent. This question on fairness is only applicable to those who belong to this line of mind/thought or perspective. The closest authority that Contractarians challenge is in the family. "Why must I follow your instructions when I did not consent to you being my parent?" We can go on challenging other authorities in religion, politics, and for those who believe in God, challenging God's authority. Creating or taking human life is justifiable or unjustifiable depending on two sets of beliefs. The general principle of atheism suggests that neither creating nor taking human life is a decision of morality. We can do as we wish, with worldly consequences, as only this worldly law exists. For those who believe that the Unseen World does exist, they believe that the worldly law works in tandem with the first law (mentioned in number three). Hence, the answer should be sourced from that other law as well.

5. ***Is there a true selfless act of kindness? If helping others makes us feel good about ourselves, are we truly selfless?***

According to Utilitarian thinking, people would not act without calculating pleasure and pain in order to maximise their own interest. In fact, they argued that those who believe in heaven and hellfire make decisions based on the calculation of the pleasure in heaven and the pain in hellfire. We are made of two beings: finite and infinite. Our finite selves guide all of our decisions; therefore, no act is truly selfless. Humans should explore their infinite self, hoping that at one point they would be able to perform a truly selfless act. However, that does not mean that they should stop with the "unselfless" acts prior to reaching the point of selflessness.

6. ***Philosophy is indeed an interesting area of study. At times, I feel like it overlaps with religion a lot and I have to refrain myself from digging further. As an academician and a Muslim, what is your advice or rather tips to demarcate the two? Some questions may lead to questioning faith; how do you draw the line?***

(Thank you. I will explain the following from the way I understand Islam.)

Academicians who believe in religiosity conceive philosophy differently from those with no such belief. First, how they understand the concept of *tabula rasa* (blank slate). Philosophers believe that when we are born, nothing is developed in our mind but emptiness. Everything about us is inscripted after that. All ideas including religions, ideologies, even to some the identity of our gender, are installed in the mind after we are born. Therefore, the idea of God is said to have come later, created by men. Meanwhile, those who subscribe to religiosity not only believe in the concept of *tabula rasa*, but they also believe in the concept of biology and spirituality. Even if our mind is empty, our biology dictates how the mind naturally develops (for example, gender identity). Spirituality works in His mystery. When we are born, the longingness towards our Creator is built-in, therefore the belief in God is not only easy but also inescapable. A person may need to go to certain lengths just to not believe in God's existence.

Religion allows us to ask any type of question, provided that we genuinely and sincerely are longing for the answer. However, we must admit that we are just a slave in front of the Almighty God; no terms and conditions. Hence, it is strongly advised that we must practise religious self-censorship when presenting questions on religious matters that relate to theology (*aqidah*). Philosophical questions are good questions if we are really sincere when asking them. There is a good reason Socrates only allowed philosophy to be taught to those who have matured (which, during his time, were people above 40). People who ask philosophical questions without wisdom ask them just to test the authority of the available answers or to demonstrate their anger and probably admire their own achievement, and so-on. If we ask questions, make sure it comes from our heart or our curiosity, and not as a way of presenting our ego. Then only can we naturally be attracted to wisdom.

We should also admit that we have the tendency to think that other entities, for example God, also think logically like us. One of the things we have thought of is, if He created us, then who created Him? The logic of a triangle is completely different from the logic of a circle. In reference to what Jeffrey Lang mentioned, it is okay to ask how many corners are in a triangle to calculate the total angle, but it is definitely wrong to ask how many corners are in a circle for the same purpose just because of our triangular mindset. The point here is that many of the problems in philosophical questions lie in the questions themselves.

In philosophy, you can have Contractarianism, Utilitarianism, Kantianism, Aristotelianism, and many hundreds other perspectives. Philosophy is the study of the perspectives of truth, not the truth itself.

Conclusion

This exercise (responding to questions from three respondents) may imply that the clinic for Philosophical Questions is both necessary and useful. However, I sense that it is not just philosophy, but religion is always asked as well, implying that these two are closely connected and a religiophilosopical clinic is actually that much needed. If you still think otherwise, then there is a good reason for you to stop reading this book and focus on other things that are more important and suitable to you since a misfit shoe would only trip you. It is learned from the respondents' questions, the current generation is in need of space to debate on matters concerning philosophy, and it is nearly impossible not to discuss philosophy together with religion. However, questions on religion are just like questions on medical matters—they should be responded to by experts on the subject. What to do or not to do in religious matters can be similar to advice from the physician too. The difference in a single milligram of a certain drug can tell a lot about a patient's condition. If we are unable to provide answers to your philosophical questions, we will bring them up to others in our network so that a proper answer can be given to you. You can also first follow Michael Sandel's free online lectures on *Justice: What's the Right Thing to Do?*. The link to the said lectures can be found below:

https://justiceharvard.org/

The following comment from one of the respondents merits our attention, and the quotation will mark the end of this chapter.

I especially am touched by this point you made: "If we ask questions, make sure it comes from our heart or our curiosity, and not as a way of presenting our ego. Then only can we naturally be attracted to wisdom." This is so beautifully put and a good reminder to myself to always be conscious of my intentions in whatever it is I do."

CHAPTER 2

Are There Requirements to Study Philosophy and Religion?

Introduction

Many of us may have had the opportunity, maybe not only once, coming across seeing accidents involving driving school students. Some accidents can even be nasty. Is there anything wrong with the student? Is he or she guilty of any law or liable to any penalty? I think this is the advantage being students, they are literally infallible from any kind of law. I always employ this analogy in any discussion, especially the one with my students. I also informed them of a couple of other benefits. One, by asking questions, not only do you benefit from the answer, but also the remaining 99 in your class. You have done a huge service to your friends, don't you think so? Two, we've also sharpened your knowledge and more indifferently important, your teacher's or lecturer's knowledge.

To be honest, there are many occasions which I quietly learnt from my student's knowledge, skill and abilities, from their questions and their participation. If you're observant enough, even a tree can teach you things. Three, you should also understand that it is natural not all are gregarious beings. Some do, some don't, and it is expected someone must ask the question to get the ball rolling. Believe me, if you have the habit of asking questions, of course not in a domineering way, you will not only learn a lot and benefit from others, you will also get the upper hand in many future opportunities and events.

What is philosophy and religion? Answering this two-part question on philosophy and religion requires separate sections; and it would be perhaps much easier for me to deal with philosophy first although these two are not necessarily disconnected.

Understanding both philosophy and religion naturally requires us to mention the topic of science, and we also can't escape from talking about how people attempt to separate the idea of religion with other aspects of human life, sometimes called secularism.

In this chapter we will be discussing about:

1.   Requirements to Study Philosophy?

2.   Requirements to Study Religion?

3.   Religion and Secularism

Requirements to Study Philosophy?

In the past, during times of antiquity in Greece and Rome more than two thousand years ago, teachers and students who engaged in philosophy were also involved in other self-disciplined activities. It is not merely discipline of mind but body and soul. Philosophy is not only the question of logic, but more importantly an understanding of wisdom. Of course, it is through the power of mind that people exercise their logic and reason, but the mind can be easily irritated when our body gets tired or sick. Peace of mind is needed in order to exercise our reason and logic, and this comes in people with a pure heart.

You might be surprised if I were to say that the first requirement to study philosophy is to make sure that you look for a teacher who has a stable and peaceful mind, and you should also find out who taught your teacher. However, in our time, teachers who study and teach philosophy are generally uninterested about pure reason, but rather, always other things in the agenda. What is important to them is how to get a good pay, no doubt I'm not out of the equation. This reminds me of what Karl Marx said, "Who should educate the educator?"

What should be the reason for people to study philosophy? I think not only do we want to have the right knowledge, but we should also have the right reason why we want to acquire such knowledge. The following two characters must probably be a requirement, I strongly believe. Otherwise, the understanding of philosophy will not work. The first is on curiosity, while the second is on humility.

Every day, we may, out of the blue, get struck with questions. These are good occurrences for us, because through them we build our curiosity. One of the perennial questions people continue to be curious about until today is on the purpose of life and why humans must have a purpose in life as well as how do we know what exactly the truth is. Curiosity entails questions and answers. Therefore, the question-and-answer exercise is a tall order yet essential in philosophy. Socrates was once told that he is the wiseman of Athens by the religious institution, the Oracle of Delphi. According to one narration, he himself had no clue why he was declared as such while there are hundreds of sophists and poets who had greater following. He initially had no followers. After all, he was just a simple man of no status. Just his looks were enough for people to disassociate themselves from him.

In his curiosity to know the religious institution's declaration, he went on asking and arguing with people to find out why he was declared as the wiseman. His continuous asking and interrogating made people upset and angry at him. This was so because there were many questions and arguments which are left unanswered by the so-called knowledgeable people of his time, and this made them look stupid and ugly in front of others. Those who were in authority accused him of making mockery to the established system and he was charged for inciting and corrupting the young as well as disrespecting the institution. His presence made the people of authority insecure, and as a result, he was condemned to death under the Athenian system.

Socrates is known as the Father of Modern Philosophy. In fact, his method of philosophy is widely known today as the Socratic Method. On the surface, it is as if he had used his power of argument to demonstrate who is on the side of truth or who is actually knowledgeable. Through his continuous arguments, it was proven that in every account of debates; he was the wiser, as declared by the Oracle of Delphi. However, we should understand that he was aware that he was nothing from the very beginning. It was his strong sense of curiosity which led him to ask questions and make powerful arguments. He wanted to know why he was declared wiser, and it came genuinely from his heart. He had no motives of winning in every argument that he had won, nor had he any intentions of making other people look stupid or ugly. They were all unintended consequences. It was out of his curiosity and genuine heart that he attracted wisdom, and through his wisdom, not only did he amass a huge following towards the end, but it was the wisdom that changed the people's thinking until today. It is not through arguments that people change, but through wisdom.

There are many questions placed forward that do not

entail wisdom. There are many who do not ask questions genuinely from their heart or out of pure curiosity. Observe the following questions:

1. *Who are you to tell me whether what I do is right or wrong?*

2. *Why do you continue wasting your time when you know there are better things you can do?*

3. *Why do we have to learn philosophy when we know that religion can teach us better wisdom?*

The list goes on, but from the three questions above, perhaps we can guess that there are questions that are asked not out of curiosity, but rather out of anger and ego.

People ask questions out of anger due to probably some of the reasons below:

The first would be when the problem continues to happen even after many efforts and advice were given. For example: *"I have been telling you over and over how you should change your attitude. Why are you so stupid?"* It is clearly not out of curiosity as to why the question *"Why are you so stupid?"* was asked since no answer is expected from it—a rhetorical question. In fact, if the question was responded with an answer, the person questioning would probably be enraged further. In a philosophy class, one is expected not only to ask out of curiosity, but also with humility. We have to be humble over our knowledge and experience, so that when we tell others how to change their attitude, we do it because of our responsibility. If they still fail to change, then one of the probable causes is our problem in performing our responsibility.

I remember Stephen Covey, one of the towering giants among motivational speakers and educators, who passed away in 2012 shared a story about the acrimonious relationship between father and son in which he's dealing with, who lamented and condemned his son, and the following are some of the questions spouted by his father: "*I do not understand my son. Really, I just do not understand. I have told him more than a thousand times, but he just would not listen. I do not know how I can understand him.*"

With his wisdom, Stephen Covey said somewhere along the following: "*You have been telling your son more than a thousand times, yet he would not listen. And you do not understand him, but you really want to understand. Wait a minute, if we want to understand someone, should we not be the one listening to them? Should we not allow them to tell us what their problem is, rather than continuously telling them. My idea is that you sincerely talk to your son, and I mean sincerely, ask him to tell you what it is that he wants to tell you, and try to learn not to keep on telling him what you want to tell him. That is, if you really want to understand him.*"

Questions that are asked out of anger may be easily

traceable, but not necessarily easily correctable. People with authority such as fathers, teachers, lecturers; among many things always forget to be humble when dealing with others, including when they respond to the questions of others. This brings us to the question of ego. In fact, many questions, especially philosophical ones, are questions that are directed out of ego. Sometimes, the ego is so large, larger than the size of the planet. More often than not, one's ego would only invite another's ego, and nothing philosophical is learned from the battle of egos. Each of them just wants to make the other look ugly, and they want to emerge victorious. This is the significant problem that we must observe and be aware of when throwing in questions.

There is one type of philosophy called Contractarianism where ideas such as rights, consent, and choice flow in its philosophy. Some of the above questions carry the element of Philosophical Contractarianism. People can go on questioning authorities rather than asking questions out of curiosity to know why authorities have developed and become so important. Allow me to provide an example for two types of questions, one regarding family and another on religion, to demonstrate how problematic this philosophy can be.

"Why must I obey my parents' instructions (instead of disagreeing with them if I know that I am in the right) when I was not given the right to choose my parents in the first place?"

It is developed knowingly or unknowingly unto contemporary human minds based on the logic of consent.

The idea of consent is important. However, when we are so obsessed with it, we tend to forget the philosophy of duty and responsibility. Saying everything is about our rights and everything must be based on our consent would not bring anything good towards our family, community, and country. What good would the rights you have as a son or daughter, or even as a father/mother or husband/wife in your family be if you no longer have a family? In other words, rights do not exist independently with any institution that we are in. Therefore, we need to respect the institution and perform our duty if we want the institution to remain intact.

I came across a mind-boggling question. It relates to religiosity, and this question will act as an example for problems regarding questions on religion. Why must I bother to do good things or to obey God if my destiny has been predetermined by Him, and He already knows what will happen to me in future.

I think the question was not only asked out of ego, but probably also out of anger, therefore the ego and anger must be treated and the person who uttered the question should be responded with care and empathy.

There must be a reason why the person asked such a

question. Thus, we should not be quick to blame the person, but instead try to understand the reason behind why such a question was uttered. By understanding the reason, we enable the person who had uttered the question to feel that they are understood, and by sincerely and honestly trying to understand the question as well as the person, the anger that rages (if it is true that it was uttered out anger) within them will gradually and naturally subside.

However, although their ego may not subside together with their anger—with love and compassion—ego can be changed in its base. This is not an easy thing and is surely enough not an overnight process. After all, Rome wasn't built in a day. Someone who is really loving and compassionate, with ego that is refined at its base, can speak from soul to soul, and this is not something a person like me and you can deal with.

Requirements to Study Religion?

As a general rule, the requirements to study religion is indifferently similar to understanding philosophy. When it comes to religion, checking your teacher's background, knowledge, and experience on religion, including who taught them is more important.

Religion is about belief. The belief that we are not just finite beings but also infinite. The finite part of ourselves is the body and mind, while the infinite side of us is the soul. It is through the exercise of soul purification that people draw closer to the Almighty God, implying that in any attempt to understand religion, the individual must first believe that God exists. I have to make a caveat here and state that understanding religion and believing or practising religion are two different things. Understanding religion is not a prerequisite to being religious, but only the activity of the mind. The act of believing and performing religious practices such as prayers and meditation is what makes someone religious. Therefore, if it is only through reading, debating, and arguing, one must not expect to become a religious person. At best, it can make someone feel good about their own religion, and at worst, feel unnecessary evil with regards to other people's religion.

Analogous to such an explanation is expecting someone to perform a refined banana kick or a curved shot in soccer only by the means of reading or attending lectures. Sure, reading can make one knowledgeable since they know theoretically the physics of performing such a kick. However, until and only until that person goes to the field to practise, with the advantage of talent, he can be Roberto Carlos, David Beckham, and the like. With that said, believing solely in God is a discussion at the metaphysical level. Metaphysics, simply put, is beyond physics. However, philosophers may have different takes when explaining metaphysics as opposed to a religious person. Not all philosophers, especially among the atheists, believe that the unseen or metaphysical world exists. For them, it is but superstitious at best.

One must understand that without such concepts of soul, God, and metaphysics, one cannot appreciate why some people become religious. The second requirement to advance our understanding of religion is to empty our minds with the earlier mentioned emotions which are ego, anger, and hatred—fancying that we possess sufficient knowledge and commending our own achievements. How can we expect to get water from others if we come to them with an already filled cup? It is only logical that we empty our cups if we genuinely want to acquire water from others, else they would be pouring into a full cup, and none of that pristine water can we acquire, wasting their effort and time. Emptying our minds does not make us a religious person, and we have made it clear earlier that only in the actual field, through rigorous training, can we become a banana kicker. Essentially, if we clear our minds, there would be plenty of room for new knowledge to foster in our brain without removing the existing knowledge, but rather enhancing it.

The question of which religion is the true religion is not

a question which can be answered at the only mind level. The mind cannot speak to the soul, and vice versa. Therefore, answers to the question of which religion is the true religion depends on to whom you ask the question. If you were to ask me, I would definitely say that my religion is the true religion in all my body, my mind and my heart, that there is no God but Allah and Muhammad is the messenger of Allah and questions on soul, God, and metaphysics are not to be settled here in this world and if we get too extreme with our conviction and opinions, a potential war would always be around the corner. There is no good reason to debate on the matter. In fact, I should expect the same answer if I were to ask others the question. Similar questions would only linger at the mind and bring no benefit to the human soul. This is an important prerequisite to make someone not only well-versed in religion, but also increase their respect towards other people as human beings. The message here is that certainly, there are things which we can ask when it comes to religion.

Allow me to tell you about my own prejudice. I think that it would be better not to try and objectively compare one religion to another because I believe that it is dissimilar to comparing an apple with another apple. However, if you think that it is in fact similar, then that is fine; that is your own opinion. Nevertheless, the problem with comparing our own religion to others is always the issue of bias. I am not saying that being biased is always bad, since everyone is biased after all. In fact, even scientists and philosophers have their own bias too. As a matter of fact, technically, computers or handphones will develop based on bias as well—Apple, Samsung, and Lenovo work with different biases. Thus, what can we expect from humans?

Another issue with people comparing religions is that each of them would look at the ideal form of their teaching and compare it with the reality of how people in different religions are. If you think you really want to make a comparison, you have to compare between the ideal of your religion and the ideal of the religion you are comparing it with, so at least it would be methodologically sound. If comparison between religions is workable, then it is also probably possible to compare religion and philosophy by looking at certain traits or characteristics. Then again, we have to compare the ideal teachings in both traditions, not to compare our own ideal with the reality of the other. However, unfortunately, notice how in reality many philosophers and religious preachers compare the ideals of their religion with the practice of the others.

Many religious people demonstrate the important dimension of morality in their teachings by referring to the immorality of the people in the West. This is absolutely incorrect methodologically. If religious people such as religious Muslims or Christians were to compare with Western teachings, the comparison should be made with the philosophy of Kantianism or Utilitarianism at their ideal level, then only would this comparison perhaps be much more similar to comparing an apple to another apple. When observing the immorality of the people in the West, they should also observe the people among their own religion, whether they are really following the teaching or are they just indifferently immoral as well. Such is the closest circumstance to the comparison of an apple to another apple. After all, how people act and what they do does not always necessarily translate to what a certain belief or ideology promotes to its followers.

I have indicated at the outset that philosophy and religion are interconnected with science and secularism.

Religion and Secularism

Secular, secularisation and secularism are concepts which negate the importance of the idea of God. Before we begin our discussion in this part, it is very important to understand that the effects of science in the practice of religion are not so impactful to religions such as Judaism, Islam, and Hinduism, as well as other quasi-religions such as Buddhism,

Jainism, Confucianism, and Shintoism, when compared to its weight on Christianity. This is so because the ideas of science and secularism were developed in Europe, which has for long belonged to the Christian community. Although it is true that religiosity declined in the West among those who belonged to the Christian faith, especially when measured in terms of Church attendance, but this is not really the case for other religions.

For those who are familiar with Islamic history, there was a period between the 9th and the 14th century called the Golden Age, in which science and religion went hand in hand, and even philosophy prospered in conjunction. However, the Muslims failed to wake up and stand their ground when their land was brutally damaged by the Mongols. People such as Genghis Khan and Hulagu Khan completely destroyed their land and the gradual destruction of their civilisation followed soon after, not to mention the crusades with the Christians further catalysed this destruction. Internal problems such as refusing Western technology, coupled with rejecting modern science and philosophy, made the Muslims fall behind even further. Only recently did the Muslims discover rationality inside their own religion, a goal which had been trapped for many centuries. The Muslims began to sacralise what they see as impure, especially morality from the West, to make it pure, and Islamic banking, Islamic economy, and other Islamic institutions were developed in the process. Concomitantly, other religions, especially among the Eastern religions, continued to find the inner strength of their own teachings as a way to respond to what is the so-called Western Immorality. However, it does not mean that atheism and secularism is no longer influential in the Muslim or other religious societies.

We shall move towards the discussion of how some people believe in God, while some do not. I must repeat here that we will only discuss the topic at the mind level, because it is through His mystery that such a category of people exists in this world.

Did the Greeks believe in God? They do believe in the natural God, meaning that we are by nature longing towards believing in God. Although at a day-to-day level, they believe in many Gods and Goddesses. Among philosophers, they believe in the concept of The One.

When science became the order of the day in Europe during the 16th and 17th centuries, religion became a subject of doubt. Mathematician turned philosopher; Rene Descartes (1596-1650) was among the first intellectual atheists who presented the concept of doubt. I think I shouldn't use the term atheists. After all, the term would only be appropriately used for people who come two hundred years after him. I should mention him as a natural philosopher, if he was not a person who belonged to a class of natural theologians. He believed that everything is untrue and is only true if we can remove the doubt. In the event of trying to find out whether an apple inside a basket is rotten or not, it is wise to create doubt that some of them are rotten. We check one by one until we are sure that all of them are not rotten, then only do we know that they are all in good condition, and the doubt of its condition is removed. This technique is influential even till the present. People doubt that the soul, God, and metaphysics exist. Since no one can prove that they exist, therefore they remain doubtful.

Whatever the case may be, there is much research which indicates that, at least until 2007, the world was populated with more religious people. Regardless of the explanation, this is factual. One of the explanations is that it is due to the fertility rate. Religious people tend to have more children, and many of the children of religious people continue the tradition. When philosophers began to admit that there was nothing in this world that is not subjected to doubt, they also began to look for other ways of life that are better for humanity. It is true that by checking every single apple in the basket we can be certain that all of them are in good condition, however another type of doubt exists because we do not know how the inside of the apples are. We only know of its exterior quality. Therefore, the first method of doubt fails. Since we cannot be certain just by checking the exterior quality, we might have to taste them one by one instead. However, who is going to taste all of them, and what becomes of their quality after they have been tasted and contaminated. Plus, we are only able to taste the part of the apple that is bitten, not its whole. Therefore, the whole systematic doubt prevention method collapses.

Religions are now measured or examined in terms of their utility rather than authenticity. Since there is much research which indicates that religiosity increases happiness or utility, the idea of religiosity gains attraction. In fact, there is evidence that suggests secular people live more dolefully than religious people. A strange data on suicidal tendency suggests that people should be more worried about themselves rather than terrorist attacks, owing to the fact that the rates of people committing suicide are higher than those who have perished under the hands of terrorists. However, Ronald Inglehart, the same person who discovered that the world is populated by mostly religious people, recently discovered that there is a sudden decline in religiosity. He pointed towards two norms, the pro-fertility norm and individual choice norm. Pro-fertility is a concept which believes in marriage, and the concept of marriage or family is very important in many religious understandings. However, the concept of choice gained its popularity, especially in the West, at least within the past two decades.

We mentioned in our previous section on the topic of Philosophical Contractarianism, in which the logic of rights, choice, and consent overflows in its paradigm. I have already discussed some of the problems that would manifest if people were to be so obsessed over the idea of choice, consent, and rights, by giving the example that there would be no point in having rights or choice in family when the family collapses in return. What is the point in having family rights when there is no family? What is the point of enacting laws in a country without people? Plus, individual choice also allows the person to be religious, but for the younger generation in the West, it is not regarded as a good or smart choice.

Science and secularism contribute to the debate on equality and freedom, and this debate has developed under the umbrella of liberalism. While it is true that humans benefit extraordinarily from science and technology, it is becoming noticeable that liberalism, despite their emphasis on equality and freedom, is becoming less tolerant to religious adherents, especially if you observe some countries in Europe such as France.

Conclusion

Clearly, there are too many things that we've discussed in this chapter and probably shouldn't expect you to absorb any more in this concluding part. Rather, let us recall the following points.

1. Start with good intentions in any undertaking that we engage in. In studying philosophy and religion, curiosity and humility should be one's most virtuous characters.

2. Ask questions if you really want to know the answer. Don't succumb to your ego, anger, and hatred. Asking others with this sort of negative energy will only breed other negative energies.

3. While philosophy works at the mind activity level, this is not so in the case of religion. It requires activities at the heart or soul level. It is mystical. Hence, it is not only an understanding of it that is necessary but experiencing the presence of divinity might make you sufficient with it.

CHAPTER 3

What Can We
Learn from
Studying
Philosophy and
Religion?

Introduction

Like my family members and close friends, I studied religion first and philosophy last after studying other subjects. This is normal among those in the God-believing society. For atheists, it is probable that they learned science, followed by philosophy, and if by chance, religion. For some, it is only by chance that those belonging to a religious society would end up studying philosophy.

For some strange reasons, I had a taste for philosophy at an early age, probably around the age of 12. However, my idea of philosophy at that time was at best primitive. It has only been just 15 years that I am passionate about the study of philosophy, especially political philosophy.

What exactly do we learn when we study philosophy? We will also try to discuss what we learn when we study religion. Following that, I like to share not so much facts and figures, but rather a story on how I feel about the idea of atheism, and how the new atheism developed not necessarily from science, but some radical elements in understanding religion.

In this chapter we will be discussing about:

1. Studying Philosophy

2. Studying Religion

3. Atheism

Studying Philosophy

To begin, we must first understand that even though everyone believes in the idea of body and mind, not everyone believes in the idea of the soul. Although there are many philosophers that think that the existence of the soul is only at best probabilistic, it does not mean that all of them completely reject the idea of God's existence.

If one of the requirements of getting physically healthy is to exercise, then exercising our minds is one of the techniques to make them more powerful. Questioning in search of better explanations is one of the methods which can be employed to exercise our minds.

Why should we ask about life? Perhaps the answer is ever so simple: to get to know about it better. If you are hesitant to ask questions, you will be lost. You will not find out how beneficial it would have been had you asked these questions unless you do, as you miss 100% of the shots that you do not take. However, this is not what philosophers meant when they tell us to keep asking questions. For them, we have to ask because we have to examine our lives to know if we are living it the right way, or instead are just trapped by problems in a bad or unexamined life. In philosophy, a good life is an examined life, and an examined life is a happy life. They use the term *"eudaimonia"* to reflect the idea of happiness.

Unlike modern philosophy, classical philosophy of the Greeks and Romans believed in the existence of the metaphysical world. Simplifying their philosophy massively, they believe that the idea of happiness resides at the metaphysical level. Humans must follow the universal idea, and it can only be realised with the power of rationality. However, with the end of feudalism in Europe, new branches of philosophy began and people no longer subscribed to the idea of the metaphysical world. Instead, they believed that through the power of reasoning, we can argue about what should be a good life.

Observe the following questions:

1. Should we lie to our parents if we know that by telling the truth concerning one of their secrets, the consequence would be a divorce? To put it differently, by telling a lie, we know they will continue living together as usual.

2. Is it right for John Doe to steal medicine if he knows it can cure his ailing wife, who is taking care of five children? In short, is it okay to perform a bad act in order to save many?

3. Imagine a situation where an infectious and deadly disease had spread on an island and must be contained, otherwise it would affect the entire world. Is it okay to kill everyone on the island in order to save the entire world?

These are questions that philosophers throw to their audience and students in order to help them exercise their brains. These three questions are on the matter of ethics; namely lying, stealing, and killing. I myself was first introduced to these kinds of questions by a Harvard Professor Michael Sandel. His online lectures in a series titled *Justice: What's the Right Thing To Do?* are available for free. He has also published a book of the same title. Maybe one of the effective ways people open their audience's mind to the idea of philosophy is by putting the logics of Kantianism and Utilitarianism side by side.

I understand that it is probable to some of you that these terms are new and might seem alien. I hope that the following short explanation will help to simply explain them. Kantianism was introduced by the philosopher Immanuel Kant, while Utilitarianism was an idea popularised by Jeremy Bentham. If you are a person who sees these questions of lying, stealing, and killing as morally bad or unethical questions regardless of the consequences, you would be understood as a Kantian. This is because you understand the three unethical actions as bad in its essence. However, if you see that the outcome is more important, which means that if you know that by lying you can keep your parents happy, by stealing medicine you can cure your wife and support your children, and by killing the people on the island you can save billions of people in the world, then you would be deemed as a Utilitarian, or sometimes a consequentialist.

However, there are those who are Kantian but later change their position when more context is added. To explain rather simply, if they know that there is no other way and that the problem could turn even worse if actions are not taken, they will end up becoming consequentialists. However, there are also others who believe that regardless of what the consequences are, even if it would result in something a hundred times worse than what we humans can imagine, they would still stick to the Kantian philosophy. You may have heard of people rejecting the idea of death penalty or capital punishment. Regardless of how devilish and brutal of a perpetrator a person is, and no matter how many millions or billions they have killed, according to this group, the death penalty should still not be imposed to him. To them, they follow the idea of "if you do not want to be killed, then the universal rule is to not kill others". Period.

Philosophers have spent years to come up with certain laws. While Kantians stick to the ethical principles of what they believe is metaphysically true, Utilitarians take a different path altogether. They believe that we are guided by the pain and pleasure calculus. If the benefits to gain outweigh the cost to pay, we should certainly proceed. Therefore, in regards to the questions asked previously, due to the benefits of a happy marriage, a healthy wife who could take care of the children, and saving the lives of billions, it is not morally objectionable to tell a lie, to steal, or to kill. When questions are asked in a philosophical exercise, you should notice that you are expected to be a reductionist, which means to simply answer with a "Yes" or "No", then only explain your view.

Actually, it is not so much the answer that they want. What is important is to get the mind exercised. This reminds me of the following riddle, "What is the sound of one hand clapping?". This is the question contemplated by Zen Buddhists who practise Koan. It has both elements of philosophy and religion. In the following section, we will discuss what we can learn from studying religion.

Studying Religion

"What is a good life?" is also a question that religious people ponder upon. Living an examined life is of course one of the ways to have a good life, but it is only half of the picture. The other half is spiritual life, the life which brings transformation or purification of the soul.

We must understand that while it is true that an examined life is a life worth living, at least according to the philosophers, we must also understand that an unlived life is not worth examining. For religious people, all immoral lives are unlived lives. Therefore, there must be a good reason for us to really want to examine it. Such an immoral life is unhealthy to the soul, hence the focus of the spiritual life covers every part of the human entity. To sum up, purifying the soul must begin with purification of our body, followed by the mind, and finally the soul itself.

Let us be clear on the purpose of life according to religious belief, at least the way I understand it. The purpose is to find a balanced life by following God's commandments or religious law. A life for this world is a life for the world after to obtain *saadah* (happiness). To be a religiously pure person, it has to start from intentions. As Muslims, we must have the intention of becoming a pure or transformed person. It is only through good intentions that people can be closer to The Creator, The Almighty God. Whether the person can transform themself or not is not so much a decision of that person, but rather blessings of The Almighty God.

What is the exercise for our soul then? This is a very difficult question, and a person like me is unable to give even a close approximation of what we should exercise or practise to become a pure person, because there are two levels of answer that I can think of. The first is at the human level, in which we have to purify the soul physically, mentally, and also spiritually. The second level is a higher level. It is the question of God's blessings. I believe that the best way I can explain the practice or exercise of soul purification is by regurgitating an explanation by Timothy Winter.

There is a concept known as orthodoxy and orthopraxy. Orthodoxy declares that we must have proper mental knowledge in order to get closer to The Almighty. Remember, we cannot get closer to The Almighty if we have an untransformed soul. This implies that by purifying our mental wickedness, we are also transforming our soul in the process. Orthopraxy on the other hand means practising the right way. Simply put, if you perform prayers the right way, you can purify your mind and soul, hence becoming closer to The Almighty God. We will talk about the mystical aspect towards the end of this chapter.

Considering all human beings are different in terms of their ability but equal before God, therefore not everyone can effortlessly reach the level of orthodoxy. To clarify, according to my religion for instance, since not everyone has the ability to comprehend theological knowledge, only by having orthopraxy or right *ibadah* (worship) with pure intentions can they transform their souls, thereby becoming closer to God. This implies that you could be a good or bad person, but if you perform your prayers with pure intentions, you may receive The Almighty's blessings, and the fact that you are equal before God suggests that you are no different than those who are at the level of orthodoxy. I do not want to complicate things too much. However, before we talk about the mystical level, it should be clear that while philosophy only concerns the mind, the main concern of religious teachings is the soul.

What religious people do to get spiritual uplifting is practising what they call spiritual excellence. In explaining this practice, I would like to redirect our attention to one of the Muslim approaches that I know; the Ghazalian teaching, which instructs us to take note of our bodily pleasure or desire, beginning with gluttony and lust. In order to practise spiritual excellence, one has to start by first finding the balance in our eating habits (main source of gluttony) and a person's sexual responsibility (main source of lust). Note that it is not to extirpate such desires, but rather to find balance—the middle path. Excessive or insufficient amounts of these bodily pleasures may affect an individual's mental state, and consequently their progress towards spiritual excellence.

Among the excellent characters that an individual must inculcate and practise are:-

- Being forgiving and avoiding ourselves from being vengeful.

- Helping others in sincerity—without expecting anyone's return of favour, except God's.

- Making haste in asking for forgiveness when you make mistakes, regardless towards humans, or let alone God.

In the previous chapter, we have discussed how science and secularism impact philosophy and religion. I think that the topic of atheism is indifferently important, hence we will talk about this subject next.

Atheism

Well, it would be lopsided to understand philosophy and religion without discussing atheism. When it comes to the benefits of the debate between theism and atheism, I find they are frequently abysmal.

1. In one debate I followed, the disagreement started early when discussing what should be the playing field for such debate, and towards the end of the debate, many foul words and curses were thrown at each other. I find such debates are often just a battle of ego, and do not make the world a better place for us. I'm sharing a few facts on matters concerning science, philosophy, and religion which I think are useful. Majority of scientists and philosophers are not atheist, but rather deists who believe in the idea of God as the primary cause of existence, but have no interest in the worldly things He had perfectly created.

2. Science and religion in most parts of history are not antagonistic. Although there are a few intellectuals who are antagonists.

Science really challenged religion, as names such as Newton and Galileo gained prominence. Back then, although they disagreed with the mystical aspect of religion, they still upheld many principles of theology. We can call the scientists of the 16th century as natural theologists or philosophers. Nick Spencer has said that Newton belongs to the group of natural theologians, and he was among the early foundations of Protestantism while Galileo in many parts of his life worked in concerts with the church. We did mention names such as Descartes and Hume, who use empirical approaches in understanding the natural world. They were natural philosophers and shouldn't be understood as atheists.

However, we could call them agnostics (not-knower). In general, those who are agnostic care less about the idea of God but are really interested in the idea of natural law. You may be interested to know about the Philosopher God as written by Plato and Aristotle, and there is a book about this written by James Hannam. Undoubtedly, science and philosophy, which originated from the Greeks, moved towards the East first in the Abbasid Caliphate in Baghdad before its flank movement to the West, especially in Toledo and Cordova. Throughout this period, the idea of God was very much deistical, understanding God as an unmoved mover, an uncaused cause and an uncreated creator.

Atheism only began to have its own identity in the late 19th centuries. Perhaps Charles Darwin and those in his circles, together with Sigmund Freud and Friedrich Nietzsche, were among those we can affiliate with the idea of atheism. Since atheism began in the West, leading to the belief that "Science flies people to the moon", it is very important for us to understand what intellectuals in the past were arguing against religion or the idea of God. The sound arguments mostly came from intellectuals in France and in the United Kingdom. However, it is in France where atheists were more radical. Intellectual materials used between both Catholics and Protestants were used to attack the religious institution by using the beliefs' own argument against each other. They believed that man has no soul and should be understood as machines. If the grand designer exists, who then created the grand designer?

Christians, especially the Catholics heavily condemn such ideas. In the UK, atheism developed strongly from suspicion towards the relationship between the capitalist state and religious institutions, making workers who were exploited angry with the church, hence sparking the strong rejection against Christianity and its institution. Although

Darwin's work was established in the mid to late 19th century, atheist arguments were not so much based on evolutionary theories, but more from thinkers like Freud and Nietzsche.

We must understand that this exists prevalently in the West, but not so much in the East and in the Islamic world. Although atheistic elements were already there influencing Muslims in Europe, it was seen as marginal, as things are different on the other side of the fence. Rational religion and theological studies are normal in Western studies on the philosophy of God. Such debates are often kept at bay in the Muslim world. After all, Muslim are more interested in religious understanding either at the orthopraxy level (acts such as worship) or at the mystical level (the science of heart purification), not so much on strengthening the mind.

During the 9/11 attack, I was the fellow of a college who had students in support of the activity. It was really difficult for me to comprehend how such atrocities could have been done by Muslims? In fact, there was a small group of students there who cheered on the tragedy. My co-fellow who is also my fellow lecturer, quickly reprimanded those students' attitude, condemning them for supporting the terrorist attack. But this is very much the reality as atheists continue to antagonise Muslims. If France was the target of atheism in the past, now the target has shifted towards countries like Saudi Arabia, Iran, and Afghanistan. Muslims are looked at as terrorists, with the hijab and beard becoming a symbol of people who support terrorism.

9/11 really changed the course of history. As the world became more globalised, Christianity no longer became the main target of the atheists. The collapse of the World Trade Centre made people believe that not only science flies people to the moon, but also that religion flies people into buildings. A new form of atheism developed, championed by the likes of Ronald Dockins and Sam Harris. Although "new" and "old" atheists are not necessarily always on good terms, both agree in Charles Darwin's Theory of Evolution.

Conclusion

What we have discussed in this chapter is only a theoretical or conceptual idea on philosophy and religion. By reading this chapter, you may have obtained a glimpse of the idea of how people learn philosophy and religion, maybe even around a tenth of the picture. By teaching it, or just as important—practising or exercising it, you can obtain benefits from learning philosophy and religion. If you want to become the best student of philosophy, then start asking yourself with a long list of philosophical questions. If you want to become a good religious person, you must start learning how to practise and exercise, and it must be done with pure intentions and a pure heart. With this, you can transform yourself, and through The Almighty's mercy and blessings, you can draw yourself nearer to Him.

I just want to give the following warfare models to demonstrate to you just a small sense of the problem. Attempting a debate between an atheist and a theist is just an attempt to see a shark fighting against a tiger. Either way, the shark will die immediately as you bring it to confront the tiger on land, or the tiger will die immediately if you want to bring it into the depths of the ocean. What debate can we expect if atheism and theism is a different world altogether? Even if we were to bring the tiger and shark to a half-land half-water environment, just enough for each other to breathe, they would only win by dragging each other to their most-favourable habitat, not with the strength of their jaws or the sharpness of their fangs.

CHAPTER 4

Why Should We Study Philosophy When We Already Have Religion?

Introduction

I remember about 20 years ago when I was giving my books on great Muslim philosophers to a friend. There were a few names that I could still remember, like Al-Kindi, Ar-Razi, Al-Farabi and Ibn Sina. I hadn't <u>read</u> the books yet back then. Since I knew that my friend was somewhat a religious person, I thought that books written by the great philosophers would interest him. I was shocked when he told me three days later that he felt like knocking those philosophers' heads since they were clashing their heads on the existence of God. I sat back and scratched my head. I understood that he meant physically knocking their heads and not knocking some sense through logic as philosophers would. He certainly realised that those thinkers were the Muslim philosophers of the past. I did not quickly respond to him, however I could sense that he really wanted me to ask why, so I asked.

They talked about God very much like how they talked about a ball that they can kick. Probably this is one of the many reasons why people refuse to allow their children to take philosophy subjects seriously. Around two years ago, I went to one religious institution and mentioned a few contemporary philosophers which of course I knew were among the controversial ones. I could sense a different response that came from at least one or two of them and noticed that some of them started to keep their distance from me. Well, if I am bothered by this, why should I even teach philosophy? Why afford new shoes if you are afraid to soil them? I also did share my ideas on religion.

In this chapter we will be discussing about:

1. Why We Should Study Philosophy

2. The Divide in Philosophical Debates

3. Is There Any Danger in Studying Philosophy

Why We Should Study Philosophy

We have mentioned in the previous chapter on how Socrates examined the Oracle of Delphi's declaration of his status as the Wiseman of Athens. It is said that right at the front of the Oracle of Delphi's gates, there was a statement written, "Know thyself", implying that initially the study of philosophy is a study of our own inner self. We may in our life happen to think or wonder why we think the way we think and not the way other people do.

I would like to invite you to observe the following statement; the statement pent that we sometimes utter or lament upon: "Why did I allow myself to not do good things in this life?". How many people are involved in this question? There are three personas in this question: the person asking why, the person called "I", and the person named "myself". Do we realise that whenever we ask ourselves questions, there are always three of us involved? Wait a minute, who is the person asking here? Can it be examined scientifically? This is the mystery that philosophers and religious people grapple with in this life. It is as if there is always a spectator watching what we do and allowing us to do what we do. Why do we have to study philosophy? We want to study philosophy because we want to know who these three personas are. Only a self-conscious person knows that there is more than one of us, and there is not only the body and mind which exists within us.

It is said that in the past, whosoever wants to study philosophy, religion, or any mystical knowledge, they must first develop their inner character. Otherwise, there would be no benefit in learning the knowledge, and worse, they might abuse it.

Nowadays, it is unimaginable if such a requirement is placed for us to study philosophy and religion. After all, contemporary philosophers are no different. A philosopher is acknowledged as someone excellent based on their voluminous number of books they have contributed, even though their immorality is known anywhere and everywhere. In fact, we are not ashamed to say that what matters is their mind, not their character. This is a symptom of understanding philosophy without really making ourselves (at least the three personas) in proper balance and in pure form.

There was an occasion when I was supervising a student, I asked her out of the blue what her purpose for studying at this post-degree level was, and lo-and-behold, the most standard answer came out of her: "*Just to further develop my knowledge*". I felt like grilling her a little more and said that sure, I understood what she meant, but what was the ultimate purpose of her pursuing her studies? She was silent for a moment before she completely dodged the question and responded, saying that she should probably think of what food she should get for her family for dinner that day rather than think about the question.

Her response reminded me of Bertolt Brecht when he replied "Grub first, then ethics" when he was asked about ethics. Sure enough, biological explanations do not allow us to think clearly when we are hungry. Worse, bad temper can be a result of hunger. However, should we not ponder upon the fact that the purpose of pursuing our studies is somewhat correlated to the purpose of life? To begin this inquiry on the purpose of life, we should first be clear or at least try to understand what the meaning of life is.

Let us have a look at another question within the similar classification. Does the Afterlife exist, and if so, how does our life in this world bring meaning or is even connected to the Afterlife? It is difficult, if not utterly impossible, to answer these two questions in one section, as the former revolves around philosophy while the latter is on religion. First things first, in a limited sense, philosophy can be compartmentalised into two groups: the study of knowledge and the study of wisdom. The former is generally empirical in nature, and the latter is normative, hermeneutical or practically existential. If we search the word "Philosophy" on the internet, we may find a definition which points to or relates to the love of wisdom. However, such meaning has little bearing in this contemporary period. Philosophy is commonly understood as the study on how things are the way they are, and such study can be hypothesised and tested for falsification and verification—it can be tested whether it is correct or incorrect.

Philosophy understood as the love of wisdom is a philosophy that was developed by thinkers of the past; from the Greeks, Romans, Jews, Christians, Muslims, and even the thinkers within the non-Abrahamic civilisations such as Hinduism, Buddhism, and Jainism, to mention a few. Each of them is different in terms of their scope, owing to the fact that the scope of philosophy is only limited to the question of personal survival of this world, whereas religion includes the personal survival in the Afterlife. When I asked that student of mine what the purpose of pursuing her studies was, that was the type of question which people have been getting asked with throughout the centuries. However, its perenniality or its continuous existence was challenged in the 16th and 17th centuries, and people became disinterested to respond to such questions which involved *telos* (purpose).

The concept of teleology introduced by earlier thinkers, especially from the idea that was systematically organised by the Greeks such as Aristotle, was used to explain the purpose of human life, in which, to them, an unexamined life is not worth living and only an examined life would bring happiness. Hence, derivatively, we can understand that philosophy was first understood as a study in search of happiness. Terms such as *eudaimonia* were employed to explain the dynamics of happiness, and these terms are usually marked by the idea of a balanced life between two extremes.

The middle path is the happy life, and it is through wisdom people can find a balanced—therefore happy life. Bravery is a good character, but you are reckless if you decide to bungee jump without checking the safety equipment, while you are a coward if you do not face your own reality to fulfil your own responsibilities, such as going for military services.

To be generous is neither overspending nor miserliness, but instead the balanced midpoint, and only through wisdom would one know where this balance is. This was perhaps the main idea of philosophy throughout the history of human civilisation prior to the discovery of physics, biology, and chemistry in the 16th and 17th centuries. People studied how to be good and refrain from being evil.

The study of philosophy drastically changed in conjunction with the changes of the world due to scientific revolution. People began to believe that the concept of teleology which premised on the idea of metaphysics or the unseen world is no longer valid as an instrument to guide human destiny. Instead of believing that there is a purpose of life as enshrined in the universal law of metaphysics, philosophers relied heavily on the power of reason or intellectuality to guide what kind of life is best for the human beings. For them, reason has its own intrinsic power as a machine which calculates pain and pleasure naturally, and human decisions are best guided by the machine. There were hundreds, if not thousands of these philosophers, but Rene Descartes stood out amongst them. Believing that the universe is guided by the law of physics in which everything can be explained through causality, humans—just like other beings—can be examined scientifically and deterministically.

At this point, the concept of examined life as the happy

life was transformed into the concept of proven and tested life. One should understand that while it may be true that an unexamined life is not worth living, one cannot deny the fact that an unlived life is also not worth examining. However, at this point, many things that were understood as contributing to the unlived life such as vices, hatred, cowardice, and so on, were only considered as such if their contribution can be supported by empirical data. Otherwise, at best, they are only superfluous.

In other words, the idea of philosophy as the love of wisdom which you probably found on Google Search earlier may no longer be the main idea applicable in our contemporary context, since philosophy from that point onwards is understood as the theory of scientific knowledge on how humans can live a good life.

The Divide in Philosophical Debates

The idea that humans are guided by the pain and pleasure calculus, especially as pioneered by Jeremy Bentham, continued to gain its popularity not only amongst academics but also the policymakers and even the public. Students make decisions based on this calculus to choose which courses to take and which courses to drop. Lecturers are also no exception. They teach and conduct classes based on the same calculus; which one maximises their happiness—the one which brings pleasure and minimises pressure.

This ideology has become so fanatical, and this naturally creates scepticism not only within the field of philosophy, but also in religion. While followers of the former paradigms of philosophy (scientism, empiricism, rationalism, positivism and the like) were given a new brand called analytic philosophers, the group that is sceptical of such philosophy was called continental philosophers. The coming of sceptics in philosophy should and must be expected because the philosophy of analytics reduces men to things or machines, and even worse, animals, as if there is no wisdom which can be comprehended by men. The project of love of wisdom which was abandoned by scientism was picked up by continental philosophers. The great philosopher Immanuel Kant stood in between these two philosophical paradigms: analytics and continental. While the contemporary generation of modern analytic philosophers such as John Rawls, Robert Nozick and the like, glorified the facts, figures, and mathematical outlook of understanding human beings, all of them, in many degrees, were influenced by Immanuel Kant who was a great metaphysician indeed.

Words of caution should be made here for your

clarification. Kant stood in between analytics and continental, because on one hand, he believed in the power of reason, which belongs to the camp of analytic philosophy, but he also understood the dynamics of metaphysics thrusted by human experience, as espoused by the continentals. Differing from both parties, Kant believed that the metaphysical level is where absolute reason or rationality resides, therefore he was on neither side. Among the great continental philosophers is Martin Heidegger. His analysis on human anxiety and the concept of authentic and inauthentic life made him widely known. Contemporaneous to him is Rudolf Steiner who believed that the world follows scientific law. While Heidegger was influenced by the Frankfurt School in Germany, Steiner was influenced by the Vienna Institute of Technology in Austria, but this discussion is beyond the scope of our discussion in this section.

The question for us is should we take a side? If we are among the lovers of facts and figures, then analytical philosophy is our path. On the other hand, if we are lovers of wisdom, then continental philosophy is probably our best choice. However, do not forget that we have yet to discuss religion, hence there are certainly possibilities of other paths and choices.

I would like to list down three epistemological issues

bedevilling the continental philosophers and see what your take on them are. This list was extracted from a work by Simon Critchley:

1. Marx on the alienation of human beings under conditions of capitalism and the requirement for an emancipatory and equitable social transformation;

2. Freud on the unconscious repression at work in dreams, jokes, and slips of the tongue and what that reveals about the irrationality at the heart of mental life;

3. Heidegger on anxiety, the deadening indifference of inauthentic social life, and the need for an authentic existence.

Upon looking at the issues these continental philosophers were dealing with, to me, they are closer to my heart when it comes to providing methods and strategies on how I should get involved in the society. I believe we should not only inform the society but also find a way on how to form the preached good society.

We will deal with more contemporary philosophical issues—like the way individuals see themselves as autonomous beings, free in making choices to the way they plan their lives. To understand this, we have to first understand the polar opposite of this concept, called individuality and its counterpart, community.

I've hinted somewhere earlier before, that theology is something that makes you understand there are universal virtues which exist independent of this world, in which our role is to realise the virtue employing our rationality. In case you are still unclear, this is the concept mostly pioneered by Greek thinkers such as Aristotle, when he made the clear argument that each one of us has a purpose (*telos*), and that purpose is enshrined in the metaphysical world, beyond our five senses. Aristotle clarified that we can only realise the virtue collectively as we are together in a community. Thus, we need to understand philosophy in order to understand whether we still very much owe to the community, neighbourhood, and family that we belong to, otherwise we may think that our success is self-made, and therefore become entitled, thus unbeholden unto the community we belong to. This brings us to the concept of individuality.

One of Yale's political scientists which I have personally learned a lot from, Steven B. Smith, in 2016 discussed the philosophy of people who think that they are self-made, owing nothing to their family, not to mention the community. He preferred the term bourgeoisie to explain such people, and this term, I believe, was coined by Rousseau, and later popularised by Karl Marx. You can ignore the names I throw here, and instead focus on the points of the debate on individuality and community. We did discuss earlier that the scientific revolution had brought together modernism, scientism, empiricism, and positivism, and this development had provided support and even sustenance to the mentality of individuality, hence it had become the DNA of many people in contemporary societies.

What gives philosophical confidence to the people who believe in individuality is very much like for those who have confidence in the philosophy of community. While those who believe in community follow the logic of teleology, those who subscribe to the logic of individuality have rather attached themselves to the logic of deontology. I believe this is the first time I have mentioned this term in this book, and this term can only be made clear to you by referring again to Immanuel Kant. Kant believed that we are only truly free if our body and mind are free from attachments. When we eat, we are still enslaved to our body, and when we think, we are still enslaved to our mind. This means that hunger dictates our actions, and certain beliefs force us to do things.

He believed that he had reached beyond the body and mind impulses and lived in the metaphysical world and discovered a law which tells him we are only free when we become the authors of our own law. Using himself as the model of human species, he believed that every individual has the unique ability inside them to write their own law, not influenced by any impulses, especially the ideas in their mind. After all, what we believe in our mind are ideas which have cumulatively passed down to us. When I say deontology here, what I mean is that there is a law beyond our senses which tells us that we as individuals are autonomous beings, and we can only be free if we decide the way we think and follow our own will, and such belief has influenced many people today and is better known as individuality.

It was Kant who introduced the idea of human rights, front and centre, more than any have done, and the ideas of individual choice, human rights, liberty, equality, are all products of Kant's logic. Interestingly, or rather strangely, the analytic philosophers who we have discussed earlier, despite having scientism and empiricism as their methodology, believed strongly in Kant's notion of deontological beings. John Rawls and Robert Nozick were among contemporary analytic philosophers who believed in the idea of individuality, of which the latter is quite extreme on this idea. The idea of individuality today extends Kant's liberal deontology, in which individuals must be given the veto power to decide and choose the journey that they want to take in their life.

Whatever the case, this new group called communitarians, believe that scientism, which is devoid of any ethical quality, is a big mistake that is ruining society. Names such as Alasdair MacIntyre and Michael Sandel are among key figures who put the new interest in community on the table, hence establishing a new Aristotelian teleological philosophy. For this group, no one comes into this world alone. They must belong to a family and a community. A bourgeois cannot become what he or she has become without being indebted heavily to their family and community. Therefore, to be unbeholden to the community and society is to be forgetful of our own identity, let alone our inner self.

Is There Any Danger in Studying Philosophy?

Well, different people have different intentions on why they choose to study philosophy. Let me answer the question of "is there any danger of philosophy" in three versions.

1. Yes, it is very dangerous.

2. No, it really is just a process of adding knowledge.

3. No, in fact, it is much needed and overwhelmingly welcomed.

It occurred to me when my family members knew I taught subjects related to philosophy. As I expected, eyebrow raises came from their direction. I probably also sensed that some of us or some of your parents I can also say might worry when you study Western Philosophy and are curious to know what exactly are the things that I shared in class, or in this case what I wrote in this book.

To begin with, it is very true that studying philosophy can be dangerous, as observed by David Hume responding to the evil in this world. When he was given the question of God forbidding evil in this world, he said "if God wants to prevent evil but is unable to, God is impotent. If He is able to but unwilling, then God is malevolent. If God is willing and able to, then God is the source of evil." By the way, David Hume is one of the Western philosophers who rejects the idea of morality and also religiosity. According to him, we don't need them because we can know the truth by collecting all the necessary data or information. He said something along the lines of "If all factual questions were solved, no moral questions would be left".

Studying philosophy can really be dangerous if an individual is too selective and takes extreme positions. People like Hume or Descartes or those who are grouped under scientism, positivism, and empiricism were accused as lunatics because they failed to understand human wisdom and experience. I feel bad mentioning them as such, but at least this is the thing that I know based on what other people said about them, especially among the continentalist. Philosophy can be dangerous too because there is a group of philosophy or rather movement called nihilism and existentialism that believe all ideas, including certain philosophies and of course religion according to this group, is at best evil. They limit our freedom so we can't choose what we want to be and what we want to feel. I will try in some other chapters later to touch on this movement. It is a known fact that the development of secularism or the rejection of the idea of religion and the concept of God begins by the development of science and philosophy. One has to study philosophy with great care unless one is an atheist.

Let me answer number 2. The studying of philosophy is not dangerous—it's really an adding knowledge process. What is the big picture? Studying trees without understanding the concept of forests can be problematic.

In Christianity, studying religion is not so much through other means such as in Islam. While in Islam religion means practice at the orthopraxis level, religion is orthodoxy in Christianity—meaning having a right mind to comprehend God. The concept of *ratio decidendi* or reason is deep in Christianity. In this case, philosophy is a powerful tool for them to have an understanding of God. A good Christian must be really good in their articulation of their understanding of God, and therefore you can see that debates over the idea of God are at the centre of Christianity. David Hume's syllogism above actually points to the issue of theodicy in Christianity. It is about the justification of God over any issues such as the evil in this world.

The response that I got when my family members knew that I studied philosophy was eyebrow raises. It is something that should be expected, in fact the word philosophy is not used to talk about god, rather the word *aqidah* (theology) is more appropriately used on this subject although the very meaning of the debate should not be much different.

I want to give you one example, in an attempt to understand the attribute of God, there is a term used, both philosopher and the religious Christian such as divine transcendental and divine imminent. You might be surprised when there are many theologians that use the word *tanzih* which is equivalent to divine transcendence and *tashbih* which is equivalent to divine imminence. This is what I meant by an adding knowledge process. Actually, it is through philosophy another subfield developed, political philosophy gives birth to political science, political economic philosophy gives birth to economics, the logic continues. While philosophy is useful, but I also should say something here that it would be better for us to also understand how philosophy works in the Eastern region or in your own religion, in my case Islam. Of course, there are many great Muslim philosophers and theologians, I guess this is not the right place for me to say about it, we will look at it in other chapter.

Let us jump to the answer number three, no, studying philosophy is not dangerous, but much needed and overwhelmingly welcomed.

When I teach the course of philosophy, religion and spiritual life, and come out with this book I wanted to defend this argument or opposition that says studying philosophy is much needed. Why do I say so?

1. Historical reason: Some of us who studied history, especially Islamic history may come across a chapter which discusses the influx of Western ideas especially Greek and Rome. In a religious society, not only Muslims were there in the Arab land, there were also Christians and Jews. In the case of Islam, it has become so evidently dangerous when even the Quran with its uncreated and ontological statuses were challenged by philosophy which influences the mind of Muslims. Thoughts from Plato and Aristotle spread largely in the Arab land, and hundreds of Muslims became philosophers (recall the names like Al-Kindi, Ar-Razi, Al-Farabi and Ibn Sina noted at the outset). In such a scenario, if a Muslim finds something strange with what philosophy teaches them, they cannot present Quranic verses and ethical sayings to the group. They need philosophy to explain philosophy. What is the first book written by Al-Ghazali before he wrote other

books? *The Aim of Philosophy*, and as if setting the stage, he then came up with a book on *The Incoherence of The Philosophers*. Al-Ghazali's knowledge on philosophy is more than voluminous. Erudite luminaries like him are much needed and more than welcomed.

2. You might say that "What was in the past is already in the past and is already history". Muslims already have a book on "rejecting philosophy" from Al-Ghazali, why can't they just use this book or books produced by Muslim philosophers of the past? We should notice that there is another influx of philosophy from the West after the first one. While the first one came from Greece and Rome, the second came from Europe and North America. It will shake the foundation of religion if we do not know what it tells. To my knowledge, we need a new Al-Ghazali and I hope that one of the Muslims among you can aspire to be like him. We have to master the idea of philosophy, understand who Plato and Aristotle are, and therefore in today's world, know not only people like Descartes and Hume, but also the currents from Kant to Nietzsche, to Rawls to Habermas, just to name a few. It is a kind of double-edged sword, as you aired your knowledge, you too can use it to defend your belief.

3. You should be able to notice that in the Western world, or I should say the Christian world, there was a great

philosopher and theologian named Thomas Aquinas. He had reassembled Greek works, particularly Aristotle's in his momentous work, *Summa Theologica*, in which Aristotle's ideas are carefully discussed. Today, as we have discussed, neo-Aquinas or neo-Aristotle already exist in the Christian world. One notable thinker of this idea is Alasdair MacIntyre, and his book *After Virtue* is just like a new Bible, if I may use that term. As time flies, globalisation and ICTs don't require your generation to go to the West to study philosophy. You can study philosophy online. Not only are there many, they are also free. One of the examples is like the one that I always talk about, Michael Sandel's online lectures and his book, *Justice: What's the Right Thing to Do?*. Even though you don't want to study philosophy or your religion to study philosophy, it is available at people's fingertips. I think it's important for us to study philosophy to defend religion. We should worry more when we puzzle ourselves with many questions that we don't understand and when our society starts philosophising unnecessarily and worse, begins to question the existence of God. Just to share with you some information, numerous current studies by experts on religion in the world, such as by Inglehart as I have mentioned earlier, indicate that there is a trend of decline in religion in the world and one of the reasons for this is that there are many people now that embrace the idea of radical individual choice. They choose to be and feel what they want. Choosing abortion is probably common, but choosing not to pay tax because it is theft of their fruit of labour, choosing not to wear safety helmets since their life is their own responsibility, and choosing to do whatever they want with their body as it belongs to them are obviously extreme individual choices.

These are slight glimpses of the reality it is now. Hence, we need to understand the negative impacts of radical individual choice, how it works, and how we can respond to it, as we should keep our friends close and our enemies closer. This requires us to study philosophy.

Conclusion

I would like to highlight the idea of teleology and deontology. Thinkers like Aristotle believe that the Universal Idea of Virtue exists in the metaphysical realm. The principle of teleology means that humans have to strive to use reason to rationalise the idea so they can realise it in this world. But other thinkers such as Immanuel Kant employed the idea or rather method of deontology in which according to him, moral good exists universally in the realm of metaphysics. Deontology is an idea that whatever activity humans do, it must mirror the moral good, the good that humans can reason out using the power of the mind. It is very important for us to understand philosophy not only as a way to improve our understanding about the world, but also use it when necessary to defend our fate and religion. At the same time, to improve our own beliefs.

CHAPTER 5

Why Does Religion Matter?

Introduction

One of the professors in Development Economics Department once contacted me, asking for my opinion on a specific issue he has been dealing with, where a person bombarded him with a list of *hadith* (the ethical sayings of Prophet Muhammad SAW) that the person assumed religion as condemning women. The person did this as a response to an article that the professor wrote which suggested the Afghanistan government to follow Indonesia's religious teachings, which would enable the fostering of women's education. This act by this person as a response to the article is such a telling indicator of his intentions. Seeing that the *hadith* placed in the limelight are hadith which presumably condemns women, what lurks in the person's mind asking the question to the professor is probably "In what way can the Muslims suggest something beneficial for women, when their prophet himself did not demonstrate such character?".

I am no expert for the question directed to the professor, nor am I authorised to speak on Development Economics or Islamic Studies.

The fact that the professor had asked many people prior to me implies that I was just one of the people on his list to look for the answer. Even so, I will just mention a couple of points which I normally do when responding to such unhealthy questions. I would try my best to understand the motive behind the question, whether it is really out of curiosity or only out of anger and hatred. This is traceable depending on the type of question directed. Undoubtedly, the devil is in the details. Questions given out of humility are often questions guided by curiosity. I also believe that any answer which is out of love will bring therapy to anyone asking these sorts of questions, regardless of their motivation.

Perhaps this short story may imply that it is very important for us to have a better grasp of knowledge of religion, hoping that the more knowledge we have on our religion and other people's religion, the higher the respect we can develop amongst ourselves. This discussion brings us to the topic of why religion matters?

Our discussion on religion thus far takes the idea of god, or sometimes I mention as Almighty God, for granted, as if we all have no issues regarding the meaning of god itself we are dealing with here. I have in mind to discuss this subject towards the end of this chapter, and I hope you can be patient with me until we get there. Before we do that, let us try to answer this question first: which one matters most, philosophy or religion?

In this chapter, we will discuss:

1.   The Importance of Both Philosophy and Religion

2.   The Benefits of Religious Wisdom

3.   What We Can and Cannot Cooperate in Religion

The Importance of Both Philosophy and Religion

A contemporary philosopher from Harvard, whose name I have mentioned several times in this book, Michael Sandel, posed numerous questions on how we can have a good life or obtain the right wisdom in his book, *Justice: What's The Right Thing To Do?*. According to him, what is exactly the right thing to do is highly influenced by the philosophy embraced by the person, either analytical or others such as continental, a discussion which we have gone through in the previous chapter.

The important missing part of such debate on wisdom and knowledge is the fact that humans are not just finite beings with a body and mind, but throughout centuries, humans have discovered and experienced the infinite dimension, that is the soul of human creatures. The understanding among scientists and atheist philosophers that the soul's existence is at best only a possibility which makes them treat the infinite being of men as the least important, thus this topic is often neglected in any discourse on human knowledge and spirituality. Experts on religion had brought this matter to the front row and filled this gap, and the importance of this aspect of mankind could no longer be denied simply due to the argument that there are more religious people in the world compared to those who are non-religious or atheists.

Nevertheless, besides this continuing demand, why should we study religion? We are going to respond to this question by examining three key topics, namely the curiosity for knowledge, benefits of religious wisdom, and the promise for spiritual excellence.

There are many ways people discuss religion, with varying approaches when it comes to different categories of religion. The most common category is that of Abrahamic and non-Abrahamic religions, in which the former includes Judaism, Christianity, and Islam, while the latter includes Hinduism, Buddhism, Jainism, and other quasi-religions such as Confucianism, Shintoism and Zen. Most of the world's population are Christian, and they are divided mainly into two, the Catholics and the Protestants. This is then followed by Islam, in which the large majority of them (85%) are Sunni, while the remaining are Shi'i and others.

Much like philosophy, some people are only interested in empirical data instead of the normative or teaching aspects of religion. Examples of empirical questions regarding religion are as follows:

1. Why is it that the number of Muslim adherers is rising?

2. Why is it that Buddhism adherers remain the same?

3. Why is Christianity declining in secular states, but gaining in countries such as Korea and Japan?

The list goes on, but what exactly do we mean when we say that these questions are empirical instead of normative? They are empirical because they tell us of either a correlation or causation (causality) between two or more variables. This means that if a proper investigation or research is to be conducted, we can eventually find the answers to all of the questions above. Presumably, you may already have some guesses as to what the answers to these questions would be. The guesses that you have is but a hunch, and if properly conceived, they can be understood as hypotheses or propositions. When we say that something is empirical, we are referring to the process of finding the answer through methods of testing, falsifying, or verifying the hypotheses.

Surely enough, some people are interested in normative questions as well, and they are interested in this aspect just for the sake of wanting to know, without interest in seeking the wisdom that they can acquire from the teachings. In short, the normative aspect of all religions is teaching about how we can control our desire because nearly all religions believe that the problems we encounter in life are related to desire.

Let me try to give an example. How does Buddhism for instance believe that mankind's worldly sufferings are caused by their worldly desires (power, prestige, wealth, and the like)? Of course, these desires are by no means easy to capture, as one must sacrifice a multitude in order to strive for all of them. Sometimes, one has to even result in abusing or exploiting others to get what they want. Every desire creates expectations, and expectations cannot be achieved without problems. These problems are problems that create anguish. Therefore, the way to remove or lower human suffering is by removing or lowering human desire.

The difference with non-Abrahamic religions such as Buddhism from Abrahamic religions can be seen within questions that concern the Almighty God. The monotheistic belief of Judaism, Christianity, and Islam implies that an important way to draw closer to the Almighty God is by purifying our heart and soul. This also can only be done through the lowering or removal of desires.

Obviously, there are many benefits of practising religion, and people who practise different religions would be able to tell you more from their own practice. I would like to discuss other beneficial aspects of religious practice which involve wisdom that is not in itself an aspect of religiosity.

This might be confusing to some, but hopefully things are made clearer once you have reached the end of this section.

Firstly, there are many who try to understand the wisdom of religion by looking at its utility instead of authenticity. What I mean here is that there is much empirical evidence which suggests that people who are religiously affiliated are more peaceful and balanced compared to those who are non-affiliated or secular. In fact, there are many data which indicate that those who are committing suicide are mostly among those who belong to families with high disinterest in religion. Therefore, it is not the normativity of the religious teachings that is of interest to the people who are practising religion, but rather the outcome or benefits that those religious practices can offer.

What should be the agenda is not aiming for worldly benefits, because in nearly all religious practices, worldly benefits do not indicate much about the benefits in the World After.

People study religion by examining and emulating the characteristics and traits of the founder or the prophet of the religion in order to benefit from the character's wisdom. When people talk about Jesus, he is commonly known as the Redeemer of Mankind, while Prophet Muhammad SAW on the other hand is the Mercy of Mankind, and Buddha is the compassionate spirit that brings peace to this world. What are basically the characters that exemplify the wisdom in such great figures? Jesus, as understood in both Christianity and Islam, is known as a man with great character. From him, universal love flows. Not only is he a loving man, but he is also known for his focus on the life after death, hence he lived an ascetic and simple life in his world.

For Prophet Muhammad SAW, his four most well-known character ethics loom large in Islamic literature: truthful, trustworthy, communicative, and intelligent. Buddha too resembled virtuous ethics. From someone who lived in a palace, he renounced the gratification of wealth and bodily pleasures, focusing only on his inner self, progressing levels after levels to attain the state of Nirvana (truth). Such characteristics and achievements worthy of emulation are a few of the many reasons why people look for religion in order to attain wisdom. Of course, knowledge regarding other seers and sages are indifferently important, however I am limited to the access of such vast information.

The aspect of spiritual excellence is probably the crown jewel on why people not only curiously but also passionately want to become a religious person. However, unfortunately, this is the most difficult and maybe even impossible to explain using human vocabulary. Some of us may be familiar with the concept of spiritual ecstasy, or sometimes strangely put as divine intoxication or annihilation, as occasionally used in religious literature. They are, in a nutshell, conventionally inexpressible in the human language.

However, we know that our soul, which works at the infinite level, is influenced directly by the activities that take place at the levels of the human body and mind, or in other words, the body and mind are the metaphors of our soul. Therefore, we can explain how such practices at the levels of body and mind may influence, if not determine, what the outcome is at the level of the soul. Whosoever intends to discuss this would have to do so either through their own experience or by using the experience of others who have passed through to the Other World, clicking the portal of soul or the metaphysical portal.

For this reason, I can only describe the stories told by one great contemporary Muslim, Timothy Winter, the follower of the Ghazalian method, whose works on disciplining the soul are voluminous. You can easily search up his name and his book on the subject, and I am almost certain that you can find exactly what I am hinting at here.

Benefitting from the Ghazalian method of thinking, Timothy Winter explained that gluttony is the fountainhead of all derivatives of deadly evils which first begin in our body and later contaminate our mind. When people are fasting, they cannot swagger or think and talk big about themselves, otherwise they are not truly fasting or there must be something unnatural. Other vices such as lust or the excessive sexual behaviours or encounters begin with the problem of glutton. The Ghazalian method of thinking, as I have hinted in an earlier chapter, is not to extirpate both gluttony and lust entirely, but rather to guide men to control them and target for the middle path, which is the balance between two extremes. The Ghazalian teaching is the teaching of Al-Ghazali, one of the great Muslim philosophers, the erudite who died in 1111, leaving his magnum opus, *The Revival of Religious Sciences*, behind.

To find this balance, according to the Ghazalian thinking, and of course in Islam, Muslims have to refer to the shariah (the law revealed by God through the Messenger) which, on public matters, can only be enforced in accordance with the opinion of the Muslim educated majority on specific occasions in specific regions. Only the revealed law can teach the Muslims proper balance.

Let me ask you a question to make this clear. What should be the appropriate amount of food to be consumed by a person for a balanced diet? Of course you would say, it is determined by what is needed by that person and what is the purpose for him having that food and the physicians and nutritionists are referred to. Needless to say, the law is not a straitjacketed law. Similar to how physicians and nutritionists know how to prescribe the healthy diet and medicine, the jurists in Islam will be the ones to prescribe the amount for different Muslims of different cases. By controlling the gratification of the body through a proper diet, Muslims, or should I say, the followers of the Ghazalian thinking can then causally control their sexual desire, thus concurrently controlling others' desires.

Simplifying it massively, spiritual excellence is a form of science itself. It is the science of how one can control their bodily gratification in order to find the balance of mind as well as stability. While discussions on physical gratification are pretty difficult themselves as they centre around the questions of gluttony and lust, discussions on the mind are much more complex as they involve issues such as arrogance, lying, manipulation, and the like. Hence, finding balance is even trickier. Thinking is very important, but it should not be done in the exclusion of remembering. While we have to think about the world, we also have to always remember the divine source of the world and how the world will come to a divine end.

To further clarify what is meant when we talk about "balance", the point of balance is always analogised as the situation of an ant inside a heated ring, as shown in the following diagram.

The human desire is always restless like the ant in the heated ring. Humans will always try to escape the ring from every direction, but the outside of the ring, which is the angelic realm, is impossible for us humans to reach, so the best spot for us is the midpoint where it is the coolest and safest. This is where the point of balance towards spiritual ecstasy is located. The moral is that our desire is not easily controlled. In order to walk the tightrope, one has to lean left and right to find the proper balance. Hence, by following the revealed law, Muslims believe that they can find the balance, and through proper balance, they can reach their desired destination, which is spiritual ecstasy or divine intoxication. Practices and characteristics such as patience, acceptance, humbleness, and many others are just some of the paths that can lead people to the highest level of spirituality.

I believe different religions have their own stories, and their followers have their own unique experiences, but this is not the place for us to argue, but rather just to share. I personally find the method of analogising as above useful. I am not so sure myself whether I am in fact progressing as I try to walk the tightrope. Whatever the case, I still firmly believe that we should practise open door policy, anticipating or expecting potential cooperation from each other.

What We Can and Cannot Cooperate In Religion

In one seminar, religious scholars from three Abrahamic faiths—Islam, Christianity and Judaism discussed on their respective idea of The Almighty God. There was a question which was put forward during the talk which was really relevant if you really take it honestly and seriously, which is as follows:

"The three of you belong to the same faith, the

Abrahamic faith. May I know whether the three of you believe in the same God?"

I myself do not know the answer, although I know that historically, as mentioned in the Quran, all of the prophets believed in Allah.

Throughout this book, when I use the word "God" or "The Almighty", I think all of us seem to assume we have a common understanding of the meaning of God. However, if we go around asking others on the specific meaning of the God which they believe in, then you can see that not only are there diverse answers, they can be so radical and they can quickly say that their God is different from what others believe in. The question is, can we be together talking about the idea of God and pretending that all of us have no issue on it?

Recall that I said if I could say something, it is better for us not to try and be objectively comparing religions, but I also encourage the open door policy. Perhaps, this is part of the puzzle I have in mind. However, I still believe we cooperate and be together with others in many ways. Let us call it the model of the sphere of cooperation. I learned of this model from Yasir Qadhi, and the following is his idea with some modifications from my part.

Firstly, we are human beings, and we are attacked by nonhuman beings such as Covid-19. With this sphere, of course we can cooperate, not only among religious groups, but even with the atheists, and there would be no issue. The next level which you can draw either in a circle form or pyramid form, it does not matter. We have a problem with atheists using philosophy to attack religion. Then I think we should make a stand among religious people to be together, cooperating on how to say no to the group of atheists, although we still hope that one day we can cooperate again with them. The next level, or the one closest to the middle, depending on the model, we have a problem, this time around not with religious people or others like the evolutionists, but the creationists and the non-creationists or the Eastern religions. Then of course, among the creationists, Islam, Christianity, and Judaism can be together. At this point, you have become aware that I am not only talking from the human point of view and religious point of view, but also creationist point of view. The next sphere of cooperation is cooperation among Muslims. If this happens, they have a problem cooperating with another religion within creationism, and of course, we hope some other time we can still cooperate again.

Let us say now, and this of course always happens, there is a problem within Islam, notably the Sunni and Shi'i divide, and we cannot cooperate on things such as theological issues. Then we have to make a stand to only cooperate within the

Sunni group, and perhaps, as some of us are well aware of, there are things that even the Sunnis cannot cooperate on, such as the divide between the Salafi group and the modernists or the Sufi group and the scriptural literalists. I think at this point, not only must we think twice on how to cooperate first and think of it more seriously as opposed to the levels mentioned earlier, but perhaps at this level, the idea of God is comprehended similarly or identically by the Sunni group, therefore there is no reason not to cooperate on religious matters. After all, we started this part by presenting questions on the diverse meaning of God. In case those within the Sunni fail to cooperate, then fine. Leave alone those we cannot cooperate with, and focus on who can. And with that, our job is done.

I have come to think that the above explanation on the model of sphere of cooperation could indifferently be applicable in your religion or belief, and if you find it useful, probably you can try it and see where your job is done.

This fact on the idea of diverse meanings of God should not be used to make us fight and quarrel amongst ourselves as mankind. Our job is to not only make ourselves better, but to help make other people better as well. You may notice people who are equivocal or ambiguous or noncommittal when using the term of God to those who do not belong to the same faith. This is understandable. You probably have realised that in this chapter, I, too am rather equivocal when using the term The Almighty God. Of course, in my mind, my heart and my body, I mean Allah, The Only One, but I think I cannot achieve what I want, which is to make myself better and to make other people better too if I do not apply equivocation. I notice even the greatest scholars of religion, even in Islam, use this similar method to share their message.

Recall the stories about the question by the professor of Development Studies Department on how to handle the person who bombarded him with a list of hadith supposedly condemned women, indicating how low women's knowledge and ability are. The professor, in his published article, wrote on the idea of how the Afghan government should follow the model of Indonesian education policy for girls who are lacking in education. His proposal in the article was outrightly rejected by the person who criticised him, thinking that Islam has no model whatsoever which talks about women's rights.

One of my colleagues interestingly responded to the list of hadith which supposedly condemned women for their low knowledge and ability, and said that if women's knowledge is truly low, then there is a good case to be made for all women to be educated. Therefore, in finding the means to an end, we should discuss and write on how girls in Afghanistan are to be given better education.

What I'm trying to say here is that the Muslims must not understand hadith the way they want it to be understood. The Prophet's ethical sayings of the past only make sense if interpreted by the experts of the past. The same ethical sayings, when presented today, would only be meaningful if interpreted by the experts of today. Objecting the past using contemporary paradigms is a big mistake in understanding any religion.

I guess I haven't made it clear what the purpose of both religion and philosophy is, and perhaps at this juncture I should try to pinpoint what this purpose is and what is the major difference between them. Both religion and philosophy talk about good life as a purpose of human life in this world. However, good life as understood by a religionist is completely different from a philosopher. Religionists believe that a good life is, of course, a happy life. It is a balanced life which is achieved through the method of following God's commandments. Invariably, philosophy also talks about good life, but good life in this scheme of thinking refers to an examined life, meaning humans should know why they exist in this world, and they have to examine whether the life they're living right now is a worthy life. After all, only a good life is worth living. I hope this makes sense to you.

Conclusion

I think I do not want to talk too much, but I want to reiterate on what is a good life as understood in religion. I hope the answer is already clear now. Good life is understood as spiritual life, a balanced life which gives humans *sa'adah* (happiness), and it can be achieved or experienced only by following God's commandments or God's laws. The God's laws or the religious laws in any belief have a purpose, which is to guide our life to the right balance, not in excess and not in deficiency. All the rules and regulations the Muslims learn under the *shari'ah* (jurisprudence for the Muslims), for instance, are to make them feel balanced and humble in this world. By being balanced and humble, they believe they are already at the steps towards moving higher, hence drawing closer to the Almighty God.

CHAPTER 6

Why Must There
Be So Many
Religions?

Introduction

I was literally shocked when in a discussion, all of a sudden, or I should say out of anger, a person asked me why we must have so many religions? This question did not seem to satisfy them, in which they threw out several other questions as well. There are so many gods, up to thousands. Which one is the true god? Who created God? At this point, I am unable to recall all the questions they asked. I was not sure whether I should provide responses to those questions, but when I felt that the mood had settled down a little, as things simmer down and the temperature goes back to normal as calm as I could, I said something along the lines of "I guess many of your questions are in a way logical. However, if you would like to listen to some of my thoughts, here we go."

I started by asking the person what they understand of god. They said they do not really know about god, but they do know that there are thousands of gods. I continued by strongly stating that there is only one god, but the thousands of gods they mentioned are just the ideas of god. Those ideas can even reach millions. There are people who say humans came first, and they created their gods. I think what is implicit in this statement is that humans created the idea of god, and since this is the case, of course it can be said that humans were first, and the idea came later. This is why there are so many religions in this world. People keep coming up with their own ideas of god, and through religion, they find themselves at comfort and peace with their own idea of god. In this chapter, we will provide a snapshot of selected prevalent religions, and in the end, we will probably ask how religions respond to one of science's biggest questions, which I think you can already guess: it concerns evolutionary theory.

In this chapter, we will discuss:

1.   Eastern Religions

2.   Creationism and Emanationism

3.   The Evolutionary Theory

Eastern Religions

I had the opportunity to be a Hindu's friend in my late 20s. We were together for more than five years and due to an unknown reason; he converted to Islam and took the line of Sufism with a bit of hostility towards the textual literalists among the Muslims. However, my five-year occasion with him broadened my perspective of Eastern religions. It is possible that certain teachings are in the Eastern religion, especially Hinduism and Buddhism, which my friend was engrossed with in his early life.

In this part, we're going to gloss over several Eastern religions, not only Hinduism and Buddhism, but also others such as Taoism and Zen, without neglecting the importance of the others. The Eastern religions are very much into the modalities of the Karmic Law.

Simplifying the law massively, the law tells humankind that our actions are a product of our past deeds, and our current actions will determine our future being. "Actions are a fruit of our actions" is a phrase representative of the law. In a nutshell, they believe in the concept of *samsara* (reincarnation or rebirth).

First, let us have a look at Hinduism.

Hind is a name of a valley in Northern India. Westerners call those who believe in certain sets of religious teachings in that region as Hindus, in which Mahabharata is the mother of all books such as Vedas (discussion on universal law), Upanishads (containing dialogues) and Gita (containing teachings on detachment in actions). Of course, at least initially there is an idea of caste where the earlier founders divided the people into four social statuses, with the Brahmin at the top who are religious people, followed by the thinkers, soldiers and workers, implying that men are by nature not equal, and to have a better life, division of labour is expected. However, as time passed by, those with vested interest took the system for their own advantage, making the ideas of caste more hierarchical and subordinative.

Hindus believe that all paths of religion are properly understood, within Hinduism itself lies several *margas* (path) such as *Karma Yoga* (Path of Action), *Bhakti Yoga* (Path of Devotion), and *Jnana Yoga* (Path of Knowledge). The *Mahabharata* is a complicated book in which its ideas are presented in the form of poems, riddles, and rhetorical myths. Symbols were used to relay the main ideas into their followers, and gods or goddesses are important for Hindus in reflecting the intended meanings of the book. My aforementioned friend explained to me that such statues or idols are a manifestation of the main ideas from the book, and I find his explanations very useful upon exploring the book, *The Best Guide to Eastern Philosophy and Religion* by Diane Morgan.

The idea of God is central in Hinduism, in which out of many goddesses, there is only one, Brahman, alone is The One God. There is no other way to get closer and be in union with God through the medium of Atman (soul). We may have heard of names such as Mahatma Gandhi, which literally means Gandhi, The Great Soul. Usually, those who were great souls are calmer and humbler people. It is said that one day, a person saw Gandhi in a third-class train together with those who are of a lower caste. When Gandhi was asked why he was in a third-class train (even though a person like him should be in the first-class), he swiftly responded by saying that because there is no fourth-class train for him. One important philosophical teaching of Hinduism is the principle or idea of ignorance. I came to understand the idea of ignorance as very much related to the idea of knowledge and mind. Because the focus is Brahman, and only through Atman the union can be hopeful, the mind can be a barrier towards the attainment of God. People who think themselves as knowledgeable are only strengthening their mind, therefore such knowledge only brings ignorance to the experience of Atman.

When a mantra of Neti Neti is chanted, it refers to the idea of "not this knowledge, not that knowledge, but Atman". I may be wrong. I would be glad if the Hindu monks themselves can explain this concept better.

It should be noted that although the Hindus believe in the idea of God, they do not view God as absolute beings or supreme entities existing independently of human beings. The image of the Abrahamic adherence, praying and making du'a palmed up, implies that God is somewhere there. Hindus believe that The One that people search for is not out there, but rather it is within us. Therefore, God is not understood as a supreme divine being, but rather, every human being is understood as a divine person, except that they fail to realise their own divinity.

Let us now move on to discussing Buddhism.

I shall begin by mentioning that Buddhism began as a philosophy without negating the fact that the line between philosophy and religion is blurred. Siddhartha Gautama Buddha (the founder of Buddhism) was a prince and throughout his early life, he was given a palace treatment only and until one day he had an opportunity to understand the real world. He "suffered" a cultural shock when he saw that people were suffering everywhere while his life was filled with enjoyment every time. The Book of Mahayana is the main book for all branches of Buddhism. Buddhism nowadays is regarded just like any other religion too. The teaching flourishes in many parts of the world such as China, Japan, Vietnam and even gaining root in Western countries. Buddhism in a way is not a religion, for the simple observation that there is no concept of God, together with no belief in the idea of soul.

Buddha decided to leave the palace in order to understand the cause of suffering. After meeting with many gurus or monks, he was still unable to grasp the idea of human suffering. It is reported that he sat under a fig tree (which was then later known as the *bodhi* [enlightenment tree]) to meditate for 49 days. It is in his deep meditation that he discovered a law that tells us that suffering is caused by human desire. From the desire of bodily pleasures to the desire of the mind ego such as wealth, fame, and power. Only by removing or lowering these desires can the suffering then be lowered and removed as well. He then came back to his palace, not for the glory and power, but rather as a monk, teaching people how to be compassionate and detach oneself from all types of unnecessary desires.

Next is Taoism. They are not necessarily religions, but rather philosophical teachings. Lao Tzu is known as the founder of Taoism with the book of Tao Te Ching. It is not known as to who actually wrote the book, but there is a record stating that Lao Tzu had lived for two hundred years, although not only is the age quite controversial, but there are several stories of him occasionally talking and quarrelling with Confucius which made the book potentially questionable of its integrity.

His basic ideas are also about a kind of problem in human society, where the human mind is governed by their unnecessary logic of the mind, making them detach themselves from their actual nature. He believed that in order for mankind to claim happiness or enjoy it, they must follow their nature. It seems that in nearly every religion, the mind is the problem that creates a wall of fire between the human being and their God or the truth, which would lead to happiness.

There are stories about Lao Tzu enjoying their nature as mankind without following any standard of living such as stripping naked on the beach or drinking contently. This is all perhaps his attempt to show that ideas are just a figment of human creation, and humans must live with no bearing of idea or mind to obtain togetherness with nature. There is no concept of the soul being clearly discussed, except for the idea of no mind.

Before we conclude this part, it would probably be interesting if I can say something about Zen Buddhism. As previously mentioned, Buddhism flourished and branched out towards many directions, one of which is Zen Buddhism. If we were to follow the Zen's idea, the question of mind is still at the locus of contention. Observe the following question: "What is the sound of one hand clapping?". Nowadays, questions like these would only be naturally answered through Google searches. This is not the point of Zen teaching. The main teaching of Zen Buddhism is for people to use their mind to its limit until it can no longer work out any explanation. Zen masters will throw riddles or questions (known as Koan) expecting the disciple to provide the answers. Rigorous techniques are used to make the student come up with the answers. Failing to come up with a good answer will potentially end up with physical punishment, probably being slapped or punched. The idea is to make sure that the student is crushed, breaking their mind for an answer, not the answer itself. In actuality, the master himself knows that there is no definite answer for these questions, it is only an exercise to make people fully use their mind to its limit. It is believed that only and until people can control their mind can happiness come to them.

By the way, regarding my friend, I do know that he had a family and was married to a Muslim lady, but I do not know whether he is still hostile about textual literalism in Islam. It is through him that I know of classic figures such as Patanjali, to someone quite contemporary such as Ramakrishna, Vivekananda, Osho, and even Deepak Chopra. Interestingly, it is through him also that I know of many great sufists such as Mansur Al-Hallaj, Abu Yazid al-Bustami, Abdul Qadir Jailani, Jalaluddin Rumi, and many others. I still remember being together with him in the mosque during Friday prayers somewhere on the outskirts, away from busy cities. I miss those moments, and I know that a person like him deserves tranquillity, not hostility.

Creationism and Emanationism

When I was a kid, I was told that there are three religions

that my religious teachers called "*Samawi* religions", which means religions that descended from heaven. These religions are, in chronological order, Judaism, Christianity, and Islam. I had no knowledge on Judaism and very little on Christianity. I did have a lot of Hindu friends. In fact, in the neighbourhood, there were about ten families who belonged to Hinduism. Back in those days, other religions were regarded as enemies of our own. One could imagine the words uttered to remark the negativity of others.

I guess the strategy of the people of the past to keep their believers in their own scheme of thinking worked. It created unnecessary enemies to create the sense of togetherness within their own group of beliefs. I do not know if such a strategy would still possibly work. After all, anyone can find out more about other beliefs at the tip of their fingers. I guess the best policy is honesty, in which to be honest in our attempt to understand our own fate and to be honest that we do not know about other people's faith.

The first time I encountered the term creationism was when I was learning philosophy, and those who explained religion in a philosophical jargon understand Abrahamic religions or religions which descended from the sky as creationism for the reason that the Abrahamic religions believe that this world was created in time. This concept of world creation is completely opposite with the idea of the philosophy of God which has been understood by philosophers such as the Greek philosophers—Socrates, Plato, and Aristotle. For the Greek thinkers, not only that this world had always existed, meaning it is not created, but God is the natural existence of the existing world.

Other types of religiosities do exist. Such beliefs are sometimes called the paganistic beliefs of God. Creationism is not only understood differently from the uncreationism of the Greek philosophers, but it is also differentiated with many other beliefs. Suffice to mention a few of them here, beginning from emanationism, pantheism, panentheism, and illuminationism.

We may have heard of terms such as Exodus, the Crucifixion, and the *Laylatul Qadr* (The Night of Power). These three refer to three different religions, and we will start this section by giving a quick snapshot of Judaism. Prophet Moses was the man who the Almighty God revealed the message of truth to. The first document, Torah, which was in Hebrew was the first instrument used to record the teaching. It is a short document explaining about the dos and don'ts to become a pure person. The Exodus is a story of how Moses, along with his people, ran away from Egypt to seek refuge in a place called the Promised Land. This story was recorded as a Biblical story of Judaism, but it is also available in the Old Testament of Christianity and the Quran of Islam. In fact, the name Moses or Musa is mentioned more frequently in the Quran than the name Muhammad.

Judaism belongs to the Jewish community, from the descendants of Jacob (Yaakub), ascending to Isaac (Ishak), and to Abraham (Ibrahim). The story of Jacob and Joseph (Yusuf) is recorded interestingly in a single long chapter in the Quran itself. This community had descended to numerous Jewish prophets, from Solomon (Sulaiman), to David (Daud), and all the way to Jesus (Isa).

Secondly, we will talk about Christianity. Although Jesus himself was a Jew, the next sequence of Jesus' followers were Christians. The idea of Crucifixion is at the centre of Christianity, in which they believe that Jesus had sacrificed his life in his love for humanity. Therefore, only through Jesus or Christianity can people be true believers. The Bible for Christianity is called *Injil* (alternatively named "the good news"). The language spoken by Jesus was Aramaic, and it is said that from the parchment of the original writings according to the teaching, Jesus or Isa is still intact, and is available in The Holy Sepulchre, one of the churches in Jerusalem, close to the dunes of rocks and today's Masjid al-Aqsa. The basic idea of Christianity is to redeem our sins, the sins of Adam, and that Jesus is The Redeemer of Humanity. The idea of Adam and the Fall, meaning being thrown out of paradise, in some way is similar to what is told in Islam, albeit having a different connotation.

Now, let us turn to the Islamic belief. Islam is the last of the three Abrahamic religions. Anthony Black succinctly provided a kind of thesis, antithesis, and synthesis of this religion. Judaism does teach about love, but its focus is only towards the Jewish community, and it also has the elements of being observant to rules and regulations through worship and fasting, to say the least. Love should be universal, therefore it should not be restricted to the Jewish community alone, and Christianity is the antithesis of the idea of love, and through Jesus' love and sacrifice, humans are said to be free. However, there are no specific elements of rituals like prayers, fasting, certain codes, and dressing, as taught in Judaism. A good example is the act of slaughtering animals, which is very pronounced in Judaism but not in Christianity. Islam provides a synthesis of those two, in which not only does it raise the principle of love, but rules on observance such as prayers and fasting which are also taught in Islam.

Why the Night of Power? The Night of Power or *Laylatul Qadr* is a special night, and therefore this night is worth being highlighted in Islam. It is special because the benefits of any ritual and good deed to which a Muslim performs on that night is equivalent to a thousand months of practice. It is at this point of night that Muslims can ask for their good faith to continue and their bad faith to be substituted with a good one. Obviously, Prophet Muhammad SAW was given a high status, as understood in Islam, by The Almighty God. Although he is the best of mankind with that status, he is still a slave in the eyes of God, implying that even the best human being to ever lived is but a slave, and no one can be better than a slave.

In this part, we will just give a general idea of beliefs such as emanationism as the primary focus.

Why is emanationism the primary focus? The short answer would be that this is the type of religion mostly embraced by philosophers, either as their main belief or marginal belief. It is quite strange that there are also many Muslim philosophers who are said to have subscribed to such belief. A famous example of this is Ibn Sina. Even the Jewish philosopher, Maimonides, was known to have followed such belief.

Emanationism interestingly is a belief which was initially practised by Egyptian pagans, and among its main important founders was Plotinus. To make my point clear, he was neither a Jew, a Christian or a Muslim, but strangely many of the Abrahamic followers also follow his idea. You may have come across the term Neoplatonism. Neoplatonism, in short, is a synthesis of Plato's thesis and Aristotle's antithesis. To greatly condense it, Plato believed in the concept of oneness, existing as a form external from this world. Everything we see in this world is an idea which is a reflection of that form. If we say that The Oneness is God, then this follows the meaning that everything we see is developed based on the idea of God's reflection. Aristotle's antithesis explains that everything we see in this world is a substance, and every idea about the substance in this world should be understood by the people within their communities. It is through the human mind that they can relate with the metaphysical world in order for them to get access to the existence of The Oneness of God.

The synthesis of emanationism or Neoplatonism pioneered by Plotinus is as follows—The Oneness is immensely good. Because its goodness is indescribable, it spills over to others and manifests into other creations. It is like a light that shines everywhere near it, and the shine goes as far as possible until it reaches the material world, which is our very own physical world. Our physical world is the spill over of such goodness, and our physical world is the manifestation of The Oneness of God. When Islam began to expand left and right, contacts with not only the teaching of emanationism, but also with the Persians and Indians' religious teachings led to it being assimilated in the Muslim world. Thus, many ulama began to devise strategies to counter the idea of philosophy in Judaism, Christianity, and Islam, and the tradition of the theologians (religious philosophy) begins. In order to respond to mystical orders, for instance the one developed in Persia and India, scholars began to focus on the dimension of mystics or Sufism in their own beliefs, and the most notable is in Islam.

The Evolutionary Theory

The discovery of new technologies, especially scientific methods of observation in the field such as chemistry, biology, and physics, has dramatically changed the way people see the world.

While the study of physics is mostly the study of things, and chemistry is about reactions, its impact on the understanding of human beings is less felt compared to the study of biology. In short, the scientific study of biology and living things such as human beings reject the idea of creationism or the idea of Adam and Eve, therefore contradicting the Abrahamic teachings. Names such as Charles Darwin naturally loom large when we discuss evolution, and contemporary names such as Richard Dawkins also naturally attract our attention.

In this section, we would like to say something about biology and how the Theory of Evolution is understood by religious people. I used to ask the following question regarding physics and biology. If the Big Bang or the explosion did happen, how did the first organism ever exist in this world?

Of course, biology is not a specific subject of philosophy, however it has a direct estimation of human creation. Therefore, philosophical and religious explanations automatically become important. Let us mention a bit regarding the Theory of Evolution and how from the Big Bang, the first organism was formed. Charles Darwin had first suggested that the first ever organism may have originated in a "warm little pond". Studies suggest that the creation of the first life form had happened in the ocean, being derived from chemicals in the water, powered by heat energy from hydrothermal vents on the ocean floor. This idea has been tested continuously and at some point, it was proven that with the re-enactment of how the environment was back in those days with modern apparatus, amino acids which are said to be the precursor of life can be formed.

I am not trained as a biologist, hence my knowledge on the subject is without a doubt limited. However, my common sense tells me that this theory is not simply just a theory. It has its own dynamism. Similar to how we discuss the theory of gravity, it is difficult to say that the theory is simply but a theory. However, since Aristotle's understanding of biology was completely different from other biologists after him, and the Darwinism Evolutionary Theory is completely different from its predecessor, one can assume that with new information, the idea of biologists in the next fifty years could be different, hence the idea of the Evolutionary Theory may be subject to modification. After all, the idea of time understood by Newton as absolute was challenged by Einstein with his theory of relativity, and this idea is now challenged by Stephen Hawking. With that being said, whatever idea I throw here must be taken with a pinch of salt as I only talk of this subject on the surface.

Regarding this, what are the responses made by the religious people, especially amongst the Abrahamic or the creationists? I do not know much about the responses by experts in Judaism and Christianity, but I do know a little about a few selected Muslims, and in this part, I would like to share what Yasir Qadhi had said on this matter, together with the opinions of some others.

Firstly, we must understand that the Abrahamic religions understand that everything that exists in this world is created by God. Every phenomenon discovered by biologists, even by Darwin himself, is the sign of The Almighty God's power. Nothing in this world can exist without His knowledge or permission.

Secondly, what happens if the findings contradict with

the Eternal Book: the Quran?

a) Everything that we observe is a sign of The Almighty God's power, and the Quran is His own speech or words. It cannot be contradictory. The problem is in the human or the Muslim's interpretation of the facts and understanding of the Quran.

b) Our knowledge is so limited and we only know a little. There exists boundless knowledge which future researchers could discover.

c) If science and the Quran do not have an explanation, such as the phenomenon of aliens, Muslims can choose whatever belief that suits us, whether to believe or to reject the idea.

d) There are sometimes unclear contradictions, such as the geocentric and heliocentric model of the universe, in which even science changed its paradigm. In the Quran, there are many interpretations of the verses which lean towards geocentric, while others lean towards heliocentric. Muslims should understand that not only scientific interpretations keep on changing, the knowledge in the Quran is not about science, but about theology and faith. It is not the book which gives us ideas beyond geocentric and heliocentric events such as the black hole, but rather more about purifying our soul.

Thirdly, specifically on the question of Adam and Eve as opposed to the theory of evolution, Muslims have to give priority to the Quran first and believe that the evolutionary theory is a part of an evolving knowledge. The idea of Adam and Eve is so explicit and as clear as day, leaving no other interpretations, both in terms of its linguistic nature and its exegesistic aspect.

I guess the Muslims and the followers of other religions should acknowledge the important aspect of evolutionary theory and see it as a sign of The Almighty's power. Even so, it is also equally important to also understand that the knowledge of biology has its certain scope and methodology. As long as we keep biology within its scope and methodology, we should be fine. After all, biology is only one of the many subjects in the vast ocean of knowledge.

Before I conclude, I would like to insert here the last paragraph of Charles Darwin's book, and see what your conclusion is on his idea of the Creator:

"There is grandeur in this view of life, with its several powers, having been originally breathed by the Creator into a few forms or into one; and that, whilst this planet has gone cycling on according to the fixed law of gravity, from so simple a beginning

endless forms most beautiful and most wonderful have been, and are being, evolved."

Conclusion

As I have mentioned before, my ideas in this chapter must be taken with a grain of salt. I must say that I neither have the specific training on religious knowledge through seminaries nor have I been trained as a scientist, even more so biology. The nature of the discussion in this chapter is only at the surface or preliminary, and it is subjected to further questions and inquiries. Even so, I must admit that I am not able to respond to any further questions on the subject which is specifically on religion and biology. However, I can say with some confidence that some information that I have shared in this chapter may shed some light, especially for those who are decidedly non-specialists. As for the specialists, without a doubt I have to learn from you.

I would like to ask for forgiveness if I had touched the sensitivity of other followers.

CHAPTER 7

How Can People Possibly Know of the Unseen World or the Metaphysics?

Introduction

There was a point in my life in which I was very much excited about the power of the mind. Ever since I was a kid, I had heard about people manipulating things with their mind, including moving rocks and bending spoons. I had heard of those things from someone whom I do not think had the authority concerning the subject, nevertheless he spoke to me about mastering mind over matter.

According to him, the mind is capable of doing things beyond that, such as reading another person's mind or controlling them, and the mind can travel beyond the physical world. During this moment, he had said something about metaphysics. That was the first time I had encountered the word "metaphysics".

During those days, I assumed that those activities discussed with my senior friend, who was a few years older than me, had something to do with sorcery. Only after 20 years later I found out that it was all just tricks. If it is a trick, obviously it is an activity performed in this physical world. If it is magic, then it might potentially relate to metaphysics. That was more or less how I understood metaphysics.

My knowledge on the unseen world or the metaphysical world in religion perhaps started with some discussion of logic when I was probably around 10 to 11 years old. It was during primary school, when one of the *ustadh* attempted to demonstrate how God exists by placing the idea of the existence of Earth on the table. He stood up from his chair and moved towards the blackboard, drawing a picture of the Earth and started saying, "*This earth exists on this blackboard because I drew it on the blackboard*". He then slowly went back to his chair. I was a little kid, therefore my curiosity began to question, of course in my mind only, does this mean that if earth does not exist, then God also does not exist? Suddenly, the *ustadh* stood up from his chair. As if having read my mind and knowing me inside out, he hit the nail on the head. He rubbed off the picture of the Earth and continued, "*The picture is no longer there, yet I still exist. This means that even if this world does not exist, God remains in existent*".

Well, by rights, I should have understood metaphysics much more than what was told by my senior. After all, I did study religion, did I not? In fact, the realm of metaphysics is more obvious in religion than in sorcery and it is the realm of metaphysics or the unseen world that most religious discussions stem from, were I to consider the teachings of religion I had after that.

In this chapter, we are about to attempt to understand the concept and activities which take place in the metaphysical or unseen world. We shall look at how the idea of metaphysics developed within the study of philosophy and how it mushroomed in religions.

We will be discussing about:

1.   What is Metaphysics?

2.   Kant, Metaphysics and The Critiques of Pure Reason

3.   Religion and The Unseen World

What is Metaphysics?

The term metaphysics was probably first coined by Alexandrite thinkers in the first century when they pondered on the Greek manuscripts, particularly the one written by Aristotle. Aristotle had a book on nature, sometimes called *The Physics*. His following work that was done was on after-nature or after-physics, known as *The Philosophy of Nature*. The work later compiled and carefully edited the monograph, making it more coherent like any other expected books and named the book as *Metaphysics*.

Metaphysics is a book about philosophy, obviously, but not the philosophy that we understand today. Rather, it has a dimension of theology, believing in the natural law, and pointing to the idea of the naturalness of God. Although most ideas in the book were not specific in this matter, it can be expected that that was the target.

Without a doubt, I have made a huge generalisation here. Putting the idea of the book more simply, it is about beyond the physical nature of existence.

It is well known that the Greeks had no clue about revelations and following this, they have no understanding of the idea of creationism, which is the understanding that "the world is created in space and time and Adam and Eve were the first generation of mankind". It would be wrong to say that they had no idea about the concept of Gods or one God, although we know that some of their ideas of goddesses are Apollo and Dionysus, among others.

When Aristotle's *Metaphysics* were taken on by the Jewish, Christian and Muslim thinkers, they provided a new perspective on it, and what else could it be if not for a religious perspective? At the same time, the idea of emanationism discussed in earlier chapter, which was developed by Plotinus gained popularity in Baghdad along with the school of Neoplatonism (also known in Islam as the Brethren of Purity or *Ikhwan as-Safa*) which spread across the Muslim land. Therefore, for many years, the work on metaphysics had carried discussions in the Muslim land regarding events outside this world or the unseen world, in which explanation were given especially on how this physical world is actually working in tandem with the metaphysical world. Every event in this world must be understood within the paradigm of the metaphysical world.

The teachings of early Muslims whose sources were only the Quran and hadith began to be challenged with the belief of Neoplatonism. In fact, the followers of Neoplatonism were accused for heresy, comprehending the idea of God and the world after using logics that are sourced from beyond the two references, from works on metaphysics and the like that were first translated into Arabic and later into Latin and used extensively by Christian thinkers who then exported it from Byzantine to Europe.

Thomas Aquinas' *Summa Theologica* had reconciled the ideas of philosophy and religious teachings of the Catholic (in Christianity) and things changed drastically in the 16th and 17th centuries with the end of feudalism and the beginning of modernity.

The name René Descartes cannot be disassociated from modern philosophy. He was in my vocabulary only once I entered university, and I had been mispronouncing it for the next ten years ever since. Descartes was a great sceptic over the idea of religiosity; hence, to him the concept of metaphysics is only useful if it is parallelled along with science. Otherwise, at best it is only a myth, and God is just a legend.

For people like him, if they cannot conceive it

systematically or perceive it without their senses objectively, it would be better to say that it is non-existent. The study, or I should say the concept of existence or being becomes so important although the concept was already introduced nearly two thousand years before during the Greek antiquity. We must know what the existence is, and what that existence is not. Cruelly put, the study of "is-ness" and "isn't-ness". If this concept is unclear for now, leave it as it is first.

Suffice if you could just go with the following: If you cannot explain its being or its ontological status, you should reject it. All the sceptics were known for their methodology of empiricism. David Hume is reported to say that we can only conceive things if the relation between them is sensical. If I am not mistaken, he is known for the term "married bachelor". A bachelor is an unmarried person; it is nonsensical to collect data on married bachelors.

These are the activities at the mental level, which imply that empiricism is an attempt to understand the reality of existence or events that take place at only the physical-mental level. Any activities beyond that, i.e. metaphysical, is equivalent to superstition.

There was no one in those days who we can call as atheists or purely scientists, at least the way we understand this category of people today. All of them very much affiliated themselves with the idea of natural law, hence the so-called scientists in those days should be called natural philosophers, and the so-called philosophers should be understood as natural theologians.

Kant, Metaphysics and The Critiques of Pure Reason

It seems that Descartes and Hume have provided a grand grounding for human understanding on the reality of existence, as if metaphysics is just an illusion. However, "the sceptic of metaphysics is probably only at best misleading and at worst wrong-headed". The person who came up with such an argument is no other than Kant.

How could it be possible that British empiricism or scientism and positivism (another term to explain systematic inquiries) can be wrong-headed? Kant said that it must go beyond the physical world of the body and mind in order to understand reality. Our mind is easily cheated by the data or knowledge we gathered, and our senses do not always tell us the truth.

People sometimes say that mirrors never lie. This might be a silly example: When I was a kid, I was looking for someone who was punched in his right side of the face. If I wanted to confirm whether he got it on the right side or the left side and had a picture of him in front of a mirror, were I to believe in the image of the mirror, he was actually punched at the left side and not the right, and this is the big lie.

A more systematic and probably scientific example is the way Aristotle and his affiliates understand how the universe of cosmology operates. Using his sense of seeing, he observed that almost every day, the sun rises in the morning and sets in the evening. It is so repetitive until Aristotle himself concluded that the sun moves around the earth. Later on, with the evolution of mathematics and calculation, this so-called geocentric paradigm of understanding cosmology changed into something that we call heliocentric, in which it is the earth that is actually moving around the sun; a phenomenon in which our naked eyes cannot comprehend.

In a nutshell, we cannot completely trust our perception. However, why can we not trust the idea that we conceive through conjecturing methods in our mental space, such as making thought experiments? According to Kant, our mind or thought is influenced by many factors—our religion, ideology, level of IQ, knowledge, history, and our society; all of which influences the build-up of our thought. With the accumulation of all factors, how can we trust our thought, believing that it can tell us the objective truth?

When I was a very small kid, I only had the knowledge of my village, which I thought was the only world that existed. Then my father brought me to a town nearby, and I began to develop a new thinking regarding the village and the town that exists. As I grew older, my horizon of knowledge widened. The concept of epistemology began to be the buzzword in my conversations with colleagues. We have definitely perceived things differently based on the type of thinking that we had built up during our years. Again, briefly, how can we trust our thoughts if it is so socially and culturally influenced or constructed?

Kant not only explained such misleading and wrong-headedness of those empiricist sceptics, but he further argued that we can only know the truth if we can be free from all of the natures of body and mind. According to him, we are enslaved to our body and mind. When our stomach is empty and hungry, we cannot say no to our body. They become the master and we become the slave. We cannot say no and do anything at all but to follow the orders from the body.

Can we say no to our own beliefs? Whatever belief it is, once we are already in the matrix, we can hardly say no to it. Does it not sound strange? That is basically what Kant is trying to say next. Descartes and Kant already believed in empiricism. He cannot say no or do anything else regarding to his belief but to follow the logic of empiricism, hence becoming a slave to them. It became clear to us now that Kant wants us to think beyond the body and the mind, and this can be reached at the metaphysical level. There, Kant believes that whatever stand or idea that might have been carried, will turn us into free and autonomous beings. We are the author of our own law, the master of our own selves. I actually want to say something ironic or paradoxical about this. No, not about his idea but his PhD scroll. I will show the scroll later towards the end of this chapter.

Coming back to our discussion, he broke the groundwork pioneered by empiricism and came out with his own ground-breaking work, the groundwork of metaphysics. Nevertheless, can we really be the master of our own selves, the author of our own law? To this, we turn our discussion towards the contemporary groups of metaphysicians.

Well, what probably is wrong with Kant's idea? In one of our discussions, in a chapter on discussing what we learn when we study philosophy, we discussed the logic of Kantian vs Utilitarianism. In that section, we discussed that Kantians believe that whatever the consequences are, lying, stealing, and killing are unethical. It is unethical in itself. How does Kant know of this? According to him, he knew it as he contemplated over the idea of truth at the metaphysical level, in which he discovered that if we do not want to believe in law, we should follow it, not to lie to others and the same goes for the case of stealing and killing. It is a kind of contract and consent at the metaphysical level; agreed upon by all humanity.

The so-called universal human rights of the United Nations that we have today is a good example of how Kant was the engineer behind it. According to this principle of metaphysical outlook, sometimes called deontology, humans at that level have no baggage of ideas whatsoever (gender, identities such as ethnicities, religion, upper or lower class, and the like) once they agree with each other on the principle to which they call categorical imperative. I know that I am packing the idea rather than unpacking it. Therefore, it is probably better if we jump to the idea of Neo-Aristotelian teleology to help us understand what exactly is being discussed.

By the way, on second thought, Kant's universal principle or categorical imperative is actually something very familiar to us, but sometimes we just do not realise it. If we do not want others to lie to us, it would be better for us to not lie to others. Is this not the familiar golden rule that we have heard countless times, no matter in Christianity, Islam, Hinduism and even by the Greek thinkers? What is really special about Kant's idea then?

If humans are autonomous beings as understood by Kant, then definitely they can choose the life plan they want independently, without having any obligations towards any thoughts, which developed through the way we conceive ideas or through our perceptions, the way we know some things through our senses.

This implies that when we were born, we were autonomous beings, having no identity and should be given the freedom when the time comes to decide our own destiny. However, who comes into this world alone without a family, ethnicity, identity, or gender, to name a few? The fact that we belong to a category implies that whatever decision we make, decisions should be influenced by that aforementioned category. Let me mention a few names to get closer to the point. Alasdair MacIntyre, Michael Sandel and Michel Walzer are among those who believe that Aristotle was right and they further argue that even Thomas Aquinas was also right. MacIntyre was one of the standout examples. What I am trying to say here is that it is nearly impossible to believe that we are autonomous beings as Kant had once thought.

Religion and The Unseen World

Say if we were to walk by the beach, and after a few hundred steps we stumble upon a watch. Is it possible to conclude that the watch exists naturally? It is probable that only lunatics or obscurantists would conclude as such. Not only does the watch have a certain design, it also has a certain function.

When we look around us, we see beautiful things. Just look at whoever or whatever there is around us. The fish in the sea are so beautiful, and the design is so sophisticated. As the biologists have informed us, it has a function. Can we also say that it would be ludicrous and ridiculous to say that this world exists naturally? Can we also say that this is just another form of lunacy or obscurancy?

By the way, the watchmaker analogy is not at all mine but was rather constructed by William Paley, one of the religious philosophers in the 18th century. What essentially is the study that we learn when we study religion and metaphysics? Since both religion and metaphysics are big words, it would be nigh impossible for a person like me to explain it. However, I will take this challenge by mentioning a few things about metaphysics as understood by creationists or those in the Abrahamic faith, the ones who practise in the East, and as probably understood by philosophers. I'll start with the understanding by the philosophers.

In what is so-called the study of the philosophy of religion, there is an attempt to discuss "What is God?" and "Who is the maker of this world?". Who created its existence (the watch), and more importantly, what is the nature of the Creator? There are usually philosophers that use the concept of omnipotence (The Divine Power) and omniscience (The Divine Knowledge). Whosoever created its existence, must have a perfect knowledge, but knowledge without power cannot transform the knowledge into existence, hence God must also have perfect power.

These two concepts—omnipotence and omniscience are concepts that imply the transcendental nature of God, meaning that it is something beyond our space and time. Even though you are powerful and knowledgeable, if you are in this world, you are limited to the restrictions within the time and space that you are in. Well, if it is complicated, let us leave it first and see whether towards the end, after enduring some pain, will we be able to gain something out of this.

Philosophers, or I should say systematic theologians, argue that it is not enough to understand that God is an entity that is All-Powerful and All-Knowing. He must also be All-Benevolent. Indeed, there are many other attributes of God besides these three O's (Omnipotent, omniscient, and omnibenevolent). They also include omnivalent, omniconsistent, and many more.

Now we turn to the second understanding as interpreted

by Eastern religions and metaphysics. To me, this is perhaps the hardest one. What I am going to say is very much of my own understanding rather than what is informed by the experts in this subject.

We usually understand metaphysics as something that is beyond us. In fact, there is a concept called heaven and earth, implying that what is metaphysical is what is in the realm of heaven. The frame of mind of those who belong to Eastern religions is completely different. Instead of understanding metaphysics as something beyond, in this frame of mind, metaphysics can be understood as something that is within us. A bit strange, isn't it? Yes, it is, at least the way I understand it.

I would like to discuss four concepts of God that are commonly used in literature relating to philosophy and religion. First is theism. In this scheme of thought, God is understood specifically to be the way that the philosophers understand, the three O's. The second is deism, probably the concept of God as understood by scientists. By scientists, I mean those who believe in the existence of God, or the natural philosophers. In this line of thinking, God does exist, but He is far from us or the universe. If God really is perfect, He no longer needs to do anything towards anything that He has already created.

The third is pantheism. This idea of God is in some way the polar opposite of the second idea. In this logic of thinking, God is everywhere. Everything that you see in this universe is the presence or manifestation of God. I remember once when I had read a book relating to Vivekananda, one of the early 20th century's well known Hindu philosophers and monks. He had attended a World Religion Conference in the West. During this conference, there was a debate on whether God is everywhere or nowhere, and people made fun of the idea of God being nowhere.

Remember my friend who had converted to Islam whom I had learned a lot about Eastern religions from? He was the one who had shared the story to me. When people wrote the word "God is nowhere" on the blackboard, Vivekananda made a slash after the letter W, changing it from "nowhere" to "now here". This gives us some clue of the idea of pantheism, in which God is everywhere and now here. Please do not quote me, especially since I am not worthy to be quoted. After all, as I have said before, this book is not meant for academic serious discussions. But it does not mean that it has no serious idea.

The fourth is panentheism. Probably, one way to understand this paradigm is by combining the first and the third, theism and pantheism. God is there in the metaphysical world, and God is also operating in this world.

Why did I say earlier that metaphysics in the Eastern world is the hardest? It is the hardest because it is metaphysics the way I understand it. It is not "somewhere there", but rather it is here within us. It is not a strange thing if we observe the practitioners of these religions, when they are in deep meditation, they close their eyes, looking inwardly in search of the soul. What is outside is inside, that is probably metaphysics in the Eastern religion's thinking.

Someone once asked me that if science will be so advance in the future, will it be possible for us to understand metaphysics, the aspect of our mind? I guess what the person wanted to ask is not about the mind, but rather the soul. This is the big thing, or should I say, issue. This is so because there are a lot of people in the West, or at least those who are exposed with western ideas, who understand that the soul is just a creative imagination of the mind, and it has nothing to do with the separate idea of the soul as another entity. This means that nothing concerning thought exists beyond the scope of the brain. I think that when people talk about the soul, people are talking about things beyond what can be perceived and conceived. It is not through the thought or the mind, but rather through experience in encountering the truth.

Hence, no matter the scientific mechanism used, we cannot capture systematically what the soul is. I have yet to explain how the aspect of metaphysics works in creationism. To begin with, the debate on the philosophy of God, or appropriately named theology is more intense and systematic in Christianity rather than in Islam and Judaism. In fact, Augustine of Hippo and Thomas Aquinas, great theologians and philosophers of Christianity, used both scriptures and logic together to further explain theology. If reason and revelations were to collide, most philosophers will favour reason.

Interestingly, within Christianity, followers can debate openly over the idea of God. In fact, they believe that the articulation of reason in understanding God is part of becoming a good Christian. Therefore, the concepts of God, omnipotence, omniscience, and omnivalence as employed by the philosophers are the same concepts used in Christianity to understand the Holy Trinity.

As a general rule, Judaism and Islam are consistent on three aspects of religion which are worship, belief, and experience. They are different in terms of the degree in membership or followers, in which Judaism is more exclusive and Islam is more inclusive. Judaism and Islam had never been as acrimonious in the past as we see them today. Zionism, which led to the creation of the Israel State in 1948, changed the harmony into acrimony.

I guess I am going to talk about Islam specifically, but I must make a caveat here, experts on the study of Islam must correct me if they find what I want to share as strange.

Firstly, the fact that there is a discriminance about the Islamic teachings is obvious, notably the Sunni and the Shi'a. Secondly, within the Sunni itself, there are many denominations. In fact, there is an ethical saying or hadith mentioning that there are more than seventy denominations in Islam. Thirdly, Muslims in majority are not always comfortable in discussing the philosophy of God, although it is not completely rejected. Names such as Al-Farabi, Ibn Sina and Ibn Rushd loom large in this area.

Fourthly, there is a specific group called the Mujbirah predestinarianism and the Mu'tazila (free-willed), where in between there is another group such as the Al-Asha'irah (compatibilists). While the first group is scripturally sensitive or revelation-centred, the free-willed is reason or philosophical-centred. In between lies the majority, the compatibilists.

The fifth point is that there is something beyond and above all four of these schemes of thinking called mysticism or *Tasawwuf*, a term which should not immediately be translated as Sufism. Sixth, there is a group which only follow the first three generations of Islam, they are known as the Al-Athari and are sometimes grouped under the name of Salafism.

Here are my comments on why there are so many:

Greek thinkers had once penetrated the Muslim World between the 8th to 9th century. Hence, the idea of God as explained by the philosophers as discussed earlier occupied the mental space of the Muslims. As the Islamic empire expanded, other beliefs also influenced this thought. The Persians, the Indians, and the Emanationists of Alexandria, all of these shared the same space. This made Islam diverse and widespread, becoming the talk of the town.

There are three strategies taken up by the Muslim scholars of that time to correct and combat this influx. First is to devise a system that ensures Muslims only believe and practise the teaching of Islam from the first three generations, in which the sources of knowledge should only be the Quran and the hadith. There is a clear hadith regarding this system. Secondly, to respond to the philosophical issues and problems that penetrated the Muslim World with a theological device, and this group was known as the theologians (*Mutakallimun*) such as the compatibilists (*Asha'irah*), as mentioned previously. The third strategy is to uplift *Tasawwuf* or the mystical approach in Islam, countering and purifying the breakthrough of Neoplatonism, the Persian, and the Indian influx in the Muslim thought.

Conclusion

This chapter stretches our mind, juxtaposing the idea of metaphysics by the group of philosophers on one hand and the group of religious scholars on the other. It is a very broad subject, therefore running the risk of going too narrow and in-depth when discussing.

It is quite strange that although most thinkers and religious scholars understand metaphysics as something that is beyond this world, it is completely different between the Eastern religions, at least the way I understand it. I indicated in some of the earlier chapters that it is pointless to have a debate between science and religion, just as it is ridiculous to expect a fight between a shark and a tiger when their habitat is completely different. In another sense, it is pointless to rationalise the polar opposite ideas of metaphysics, or the unseen world as understood by philosophers and religious scholars, when the idea of the unseen world among the religious people themselves are, in many ways, polar opposites (the creationists believe that it is somewhere above, whereas the Easterners believe that it is here within).

I would like to showcase a paradoxical image of Kant's PhD as shown on the following page.

This doctoral scroll has been verified by many as genuine, however to this day it is unclear as to why the first sentence of the Quran (in Arabic) is included in there.

CHAPTER 8

Are the Activities
in this World
Predetermined?

Introduction

One of the stories of my life is related to a problem I learnt, statistical analysis. To be certain, I am a fan of mathematics, but I don't like statistics. I always say to my colleagues that my knowledge on statistics is nearly zero. One of them quickly responded that if that is really the case, my knowledge on statistics is significant because statistically speaking, any statistical result is considered significant if the result of test statistic is closest to zero. Touché. I left it at that and did not bother to find out more. After all, I have already hinted that I don't have the taste in statistics. Even so, it does not necessarily mean all things related to numbers and equations.

My knowledge on statistics, especially in regression (cause and effect) are sometimes challenged by my understanding on how things work in the world. For instance, why do some people become rich while others become poor? When I was just a kid, I was told that those who are poor are normally the lazy ones while those who are rich are the opposite. However, we all know that a lot of people are rich because they are born in a rich family, and that is the easiest way one becomes rich; vice versa for the poor.

Such a small example reminds me of my knowledge concerning religion, which states that God has determined or destined someone to become rich or poor. In this section, we try to grapple with this question.

I shall proceed knowing that not only is my knowledge limited as really indicative in my grasp on statistics, but also on the fact that I have never attended a religious seminary school in my life. Hence, I will just try my best to do it the best way that I probably understand it, and it must be taken with not more than a pinch of salt.

We will be discussing about:

1. Determinacy and Indeterminacy

2. The Story on Predestinarian and The Theology of Calvinism

3. Determinism and Free-will in Islam

Determinacy and Indeterminacy

These two terms are parallelled with the idea of predestinarian and free-will in the philosophical and religious jargon. I shall focus on the concept of determinacy, the way it has been understood in common use. Firstly, everything must have a cause, and this is the way that people understand the physical world or the study of physics. It has long been believed that this universe exists due to the Big Bang. Simply put, nothing in this world has no cause.

Observing my own laptop, people use events in order to understand how causation works. Someone must have invented this laptop, which means that some event must have taken place before something, even the manufacturer of the manufacturer. A person exists in this world due to their parents, and we can go on listing down events prior to that event all the way towards the beginning.

Secondly, if the world is deterministic, then we can also predict that there must be an event that takes place after this. For example, as we discuss philosophy and religion here, someone might want to take action to follow what we have just said. Therefore, this event continues forth, probably endlessly. Let us say we take an event which happens next year. If the world is deterministic, then we can do a reverse causality of that future event and understand each prior event to that future event until it backtracks all the way until today, the day at which we are talking about philosophy and religion.

There are philosophers that try to unpack these riddles. One notable Muslim philosopher is Ibn Sina himself. He came up with the idea of infinite regression, in which according to him, God must exist in order to submit to the law of physics, which is connected in the idea of determinism.

According to his scheme of thinking, God must exist through the logic of infinite regression, because in order to understand existence, it must have a cause. There must be something that is uncaused and infinite, and that is God. If you do not understand this idea at first glance, just leave it that way. After all, we just want to understand the idea of "must everything or every event in this world have a cause?" If not, then things work according to the indeterminacy model.

Before dealing with debate on indeterminacy models, I would like to share my experience discussing karmic law with my students. Recall our discussion on Eastern religion particularly Hinduism, Buddhism and Taoism in which all of them are guided by the logic of reincarnation in which according to the law of karma, if we do bad things in this life, we will be born into something bad. For instance, if you're bad in this life, you may be reborn as a robber and even worse, an animal instead of human. Animals that we slaughtered today according to this belief can be human in their future life and those who slaughter animals can take the place of animals. That is generally what I understood as karmic law or reincarnation theory. I did ask one question during my discussion session with my student, what is the karma of the first human to be inhuman? One of them said, "Probably from the good karma of the animal". And I pressed it more and asked "What is the karma of the first animal to be an animal?". They stopped responding to my question because from their understanding, only animal and human work in this law. I was first exposed to this complicated karma law by an Indian philosopher by the name Osho who died in 1980. He did foster the question as follows: "What is the karma of the first tree to be a tree, it seems there is no satisfactory answer if such karmic law has to be applied. The logic is only applicable if we know the good or bad thing of the previous event to make something happen. Something like the uncaused cause we discussed with regards to Ibn Sina's idea earlier.

When I asked my friends who are immersed with Hinduism, he said the karma of the first tree is to serve mankind. And I asked him what is the karma of the first creation to be a creation. He was really honest judging from his response. He humbly said,

"I do not know the answer. I probably need to think deeper."

I understand people can get angry and upset with me if I continue asking this question. One of my students responded by saying probably there was a soul and they chose to do good things by serving mankind. Now I myself have to think deeper. Honestly, I do not know how to respond but I think this idea is close to the idea of god then. The point that I want to make here is perhaps quite straightforward. Either we use philosophy of determinacy or karma law, we will end up with the logic of uncaused cause by doing infinite reverse causality or regression or in the other case we might end up into "unkarma-karma law" which my student hinted to the idea of soul. Maybe we just leave this debate knowing there is no legitimate answer for such a puzzle. In case you get the answers, please let me know, I'm certainly willing to listen to it. Now is the time for us to look at indeterminacy models.

If past events and future events follow determinacy models, then we can postulate that no free-will exists, because starting from the first cause until the end, everything has already been determined by the first event. Therefore, it is probably much better for us if we believe that indeterminacy is the best model. With it, we can at least believe that at a certain point, someone has made a decision that does not follow the patterns of past events. For example, I choose not to eat *Asam Pedas* (my favourite dish) even though I like it very much but instead choose to eat curry. It sounds good (in terms of the idea of choice, of course).

A lot of people would argue that to have someone be responsible for their actions, they must believe that the world does not work according to indeterminacy, but rather the determinacy model. But wait a minute, if choice is really the game in town, can I argue that I am not responsible for your anger, even though I chose to make you angry, how is this possible? To over-generalise this, you yourself chose to be angry, and your anger is not my fault. It seems that the idea of choice is counter intuitive. Hence, there is good reason as to why religious people discourage us from talking or debating about the idea of predestination or free-will.

Well, of course such belief are not only exclusive to be running in Islam. In Christianity for example, especially among the protestants that I know, there is a school of thought which follows the predestinarian path, known as Calvinism. Below is a story on how the predestinarian, which at first glance might appear to us as being pessimistic about the world, actually turns out to be paradoxically optimistic.

The Story on Predestinarian and The Theology of Calvinism

Predestination is a type of *aqidah* (theology) in Christianity, and it is presumably right to postulate that theology in Christianity is a more important subject than any other subject in Christianity, such as mysticism and law. In short, predestination is a concept that outlines salvation and damnation, the privilege of God, and the knowledge that some people are already predestined to end with the salvation of paradise, while others the damnation of hellfire. It seems that the idea of free-will does not apply in the teachings of Calvinism. What exactly is Calvinism, and who is its founder?

It has been well documented that there is an internal problem in the practice of Christianity at the centre of the empire in Rome such as the administration of sacraments, in which priests were given the authority to either bless or not bless their followers. I better not discuss this too much. After all, there is little that I know, and discussing without knowledge only invites controversy.

Areas that are far in the Northern lands of Europe, such as Sweden and Germany had relative advantage to disagree with the teachings at the centre. Thanks to Gutenberg's printing, this technology allowed the Bible to be printed out and interested individuals can obtain access directly to the proclaimed word of God, and the name of Martin Luther loomed large with the protestants' movement. While Martin Luther had left behind the legacy of Lutherianism, there was a French theologian by the name of John Calvin who espoused the idea of predestination rather than free-will. I have had an occasion discussing how these two polar opposites exist in Islam, where the predestinarians were called as the Mujbirah, and the free-willed were called as the Mu'tazilah.

Calvinism became the centre of hot debates when the sociologist in the 20th century, Max Weber wrote a book called, "The Protestant Ethic and the Spirit of Capitalism". This book opened people's eyes over the idea of religion and economy, in which popular beliefs suggest that religion impedes the progress of the economy. This book argues that the industrial revolution and modernity is a product of predestination teaching. When I had first heard of this idea, I was deeply puzzled. All this while, I had believed that Europe is known for its idea of choice and free-will, and how Calvinism, which is so deterministic in its teachings, brought progress to Europe as well as a few beliefs to the world.

If there is such thing as we can call the grand research question of the book, what was in the mind of Weber was the following riddle: "Why are there many big civilisations, and it is there for thousands of years, such as Confucianism and Taoism in China, Hinduism and Buddhism in India, and Judaism in Jerusalem, yet modern human progress have not developed maturely in these regions? Strangely enough, unknown areas relative to the big civilisations mentioned, Northern Europe who were once known for their nasty and barbaric culture transformed into an industrial giant beginning 16th to 17th century right until today. In case you are curious, why he did not study Islam, probably for the reason that Islam was a recent development, only above 1400 years.

In his strong curiosity, he began to develop an idea that such a big turning point, from nearly nothing into great something in Europe cannot happen either by chance or by standard explanation of rationalism. It must be that something huge took place there. The Northern Areas we are talking about here are, of course, Sweden, Germany, Netherlands, and England, to name a few. He observed that the further the region is from Catholic control, the more apparent the modernisation is. To use economic jargon—while in the south we see the falling rate of wages, in the north you will see the increasing rate of wages.

Weber began to investigate the religions embraced by these two big regions of Europe, North and South. The Southern Catholic is known for its teaching of following a modest life, practising charity, and being sceptical of worldly matters. However, it is not so much in the North. People, especially among the middle class, or bourgeoisie, have a peculiar type of lifestyle. Instead of donating their money, they invest. Instead of being sceptical with worldly matters, they embrace. In this book, he discovered that it is in the teachings of Calvinism that makes people change from someone who is humble and contemplative into someone that is confident and forward-looking. He believes that in order to know why industrialisation began at that place and sparked the people known as the bourgeoisie, or the middle and upper class, one must look inside the teachings of Calvinism itself.

This determinism could only be understood by examining the philosophy, or rather theology of double predestination. First, our fates have already been determined, no human being can change it. Secondly, Christians have a moral or religious duty to be good and successful in this world, and they are the chosen people. The questions that lie in between this double predestination is, how do you define good and successful? How do you achieve it? Because, in order to be chosen, meaning salvation instead of damnation, one must be good and successful.

Successful is defined by of course, in the world after. However, there is a teaching that says that "For every good thing that you do in this world, you will be rewarded tenfold". Is working hard a good thing? Of course, working hard is a ticket to paradise. If working hard makes one successful and rich, is being rich a ticket to paradise? In Calvinism, the answer is yes as well. Then, you would know whether you are a man of salvation or damnation depending on how you are as a human in this world, successful or failing.

Since richness is a symbol of success, Calvinists must work hard, and the spirit of the protestant ethics of capitalism explained by Max Weber is the work ethic, that is to work hard, a culture which led to the industrial revolution.

It really is astonishing isn't it? We thought that being predestined will make people more passive, however in the teachings of Calvinism, it makes people more optimistic.

I must say here that there is a slight difference in approach in other religions, such as in Judaism as I know of, in which the idea of free-will became rampant, especially after the holocaust. Some ideas emerging at that time include, "Why do the Jews have to rely on God's decision when God determined the holocaust to take place?". The only way for the Jewish people to be successful is to no longer rely on God's decision, but to choose to make their own decisions to become successful and decidedly to go back to their historical homeland, Jerusalem. These ideas are Libertarianism, free choice, and the indeterministic model.

Predestination and Free-will

In this section, I intend to share what I have known about what Islam has to say regarding this topical tricky matter. Correction, not what I know about this matter, but rather what Muslim experts have said on this matter. To be more precise, we will refer to Timothy Winter with his vast knowledge on the matter. In Cambridge, we have Stephen Hawking who came out with a momentous work discussing the perennial question of atoms and time titled, *A Brief History of Time*. The gist of the book is commonly understood as follows:

"You cannot in fact speak of the duration of atoms; in fact you can't even speak coherently of the existence of any sub-atomic particle. You can see them as particles, you can see them as waves, you can see them as instantaneous instances of a universal phenomenon that actually encompasses the entire universe."

How does this relate to determinism and free-will? How does it relate to Islam? It is really mind boggling that our discussion on the models of determinacy and indeterminacy in the earlier parts of this chapter is taken up not only by philosophers but also by physicians and religious thinkers. You might have heard that there was a period known as the Golden Era of Islam lasting for a span of five hundred years from the 9th to the 14th century. It was recognised as golden not just because of its revolutionary progress in science (biology, physics, and chemistry). What is even more astonishing is that the scientists of that era were also religious, and it should be added here that they were also philosophers.

Therefore, puzzling questions of atoms and time discussed by contemporary scientists were also undertaken by them. Of course, one must understand that these questions were taken within the context of their society and technology.

Wait a minute, how does the topic of atom and time have any bearing to this subject? Although something seems off here, allow me to explain, and if you can make sense of the following statement, there is good reason for you to continue this part, otherwise jumping onto the next chapter would be a better choice for you:

If an atom really vanishes as soon as it exists, then no causation can take place in this world, but if it has a duration, then causation can be said to make sense.

Of course, trying to understand this requires us to have a bit of knowledge on basic physics. Let me try to tell you a little on the early philosophies in Islam when the debates over this subject of determinism and free-will surfaced. The so called free-willed group (Mu'tazilites) are those who believe in systematic theology, currently understood more commonly as contemporary philosophical Islam. They believe in this concept of atoms as part of the basis of their understanding of the world. They believe that atoms have durations, hence they also believe in causation.

On the other hand, this is completely different from

those who believe in determinism, also known as Mujbirah or the predestinarians. In fact, they believe that every single atom is created by the direct power of The Almighty. This means that in every creation of an atom, there is divine intervention. They also believe that atoms vanish as soon as they exist, contrary to the Mu'tazilites. I must admit that I am just almost completely parroting what Timothy Winter narrated in a YouTube video. This principle implies that there are no causalities since atoms have no duration. If it is still unclear, I will try to give a gist of it towards the end.

The predestinarians uphold the views of the Quran, saying that God is powerful over all things. God is the pre-eminent and omnipotent Creator. He has divine power, which is constantly and incessantly manifested in every movement, every stillness, and every event.

If the former was the synthesis of atoms and time in Islam, the latter is the antithesis and dialectical zigzag, which landed with the synthesis of the compatibilists (Asha'irah) or now grouped as the Sunnis (Ahli Sunnah wal-Jamaah). Before I proceed, Calvinism as discussed earlier very much follows the model of predestination (Mujbirah), and many of today's champions of individual choice were in those days the Mu'tazilites in the Muslim world.

What is the synthesis of compatibilism? I would like to

introduce the idea of occasionalism, a concept argued by Abu al-Hasan al-Ash'ari. To give you some idea, let me give you a general statement. A fire burns. This statement applies everywhere. Whenever you see a fire, it burns, regardless of whether it was a thousand years ago or for the next thousand years. Determinism believes that in every moment that the fire burns, it is God's act. On the other hand, the free-willed say that every moment that the fire is burning is a natural cause, and there is no way that the fire cannot burn. Compatibilists or occasionalists believe that if God wants the fire to not burn, it can happen.

In religious terms, The Muslims call it a *mukjizat* (miracle), in which such miracles have been told in religious books, for example when Prophet Abraham was thrown into the fire, with the power of God, he ended up not being burned by the fire. Compatibilists think that if you affirm in its entirety the logic of causality in creation (nature creates another form of nature causally), you are therefore limiting the omnipotence of God.

The compatibilists think that there is no natural causality, and causality in the world is but an illusion. Modern philosophers will refer to this as occasionalism which is sometimes picked up in the Western thought. French philosopher Nicolas Malebranche (1638-1715) is the most obvious European proponent of the occasionalism theory, at least that I know of.

Timothy Winter summarises compatibilism and occasionalism as follows:

"Atoms do not have a duration and an atom is created instantaneously in time and vanishes instantaneously. Hence, you cannot say that there is any kind of natural causality in the world. You can assume that if you chuck your football out of the window, God will cause the window to break because that's the way He operates, but you must not say that it is the football that's doing it, that is perceived as infringing on the Divine Omnipotent."

What could have probably triggered or motivated such a debate in Islam? This is a question that I'll try my best to explain before we end this part and I hope that the following makes sense to you.

Firstly, the influx of Greek science in the Arab world shook the strict interpretations of the Quran and hadith. Science, or I should say those who took the logic of science, used it to challenge those who literally interpreted the Quran and hadith. This hence sparked the debates.

Secondly, those who were in power, the caliphs, started to take advantage of the deterministic model, leaving the door closed to those who chose to challenge the government's power. Those at the top could nullify their wrongdoings and corruption by saying that all of it was predestined, and they were not supposed to be responsible towards them.

Thirdly, what would happen if the free-willed were in power during the time of the caliph, Al-Ma'mun? This requires a longer explanation. The Quran is accepted in principle by the unanimity of Muslims as a speech of God, not an idea of the speech of God. It has a special ontological status, which is uncreatedness. Hence, the injunctions in the Quran are deterministic as understood by the determinists. The free-willed, including Al-Ma'mun himself, took a different and strange stand saying that the Quran's status is ontologically created, meaning that it is an idea of God's speech. Because of this, like any idea, the injunctions can be debatable.

As a result, *Kalamullah* or the speech of God began to be at the centre of arguments and the debates became very intense. Scholars such as Imam Ahmad ibn Hanbal were more than willing to die to defend the uncreatedness of God. Intense debates on the *Kalam* began and those who are involved in this debate were known as the *Mutakallimun* or theologians.

You might wonder, if there was once such a great civilisation during the Golden Period of Islam, with science, philosophy, and physics blossoming, what had happened to them? Why is it that many of today's Muslim countries are backwards? There are many answers to this, and normally scholars point towards three main ideas.

Firstly, the Muslim civilisation was invaded and demolished by the Mongols, Genghis Khan and Hulagu Khan. Every form of literature was thrown into the Tigris river. Scientists and philosophers were killed and millions died. It was worse than the Second World War.

Secondly, the free-willed lost their battle at the very end. Thus, new inventions and creativities were abruptly stopped. People switched to either the idea of compatibilists who are closer to determinism or became lost in the Middle East. However, its fragment of teaching survived and was brought by others such as Ibn Rushd (Averroes) in Spain, giving birth to Averroism and the idea of free-will were taken up in Europe right after.

Thirdly, it is true that the civilisations in Baghdad and Damascus were destroyed, but it was later taken up by Iranian thinkers such as Mulla Sadra, whose ideas not only further enhanced or enriched the concept of predestinarian or free-will, but supplemented it with the concept of illumination, which meant that the idea of God cannot be rationally or systematically separated. We will discuss the concept of theomorphism, in which the concept of God and human being is inseparable, later near the end of this book.

Some of you might be keen to know, which exactly among these three was the deciding factor, but I also would like to add another. The introduction of the Gutenberg printing press allowed reading materials to be spread like wildfire to the public. Due to this, the literacy rate in the West jumped exponentially. However, this technology was looked with scepticism by the Muslim elites. Hence, illiteracy among the public in the Muslim world continued.

The Sunnis are among the majority with at least 85%, and they are among the compatibilists. Even so, if you carefully follow what Hawking and Malebranche say, they are literally in line of the Sunnis or the compatibilists, the type of occasionalistic in Islam.

Conclusion

I hope that there are some things which we can hopefully gather and learn from our discussions in this chapter. To my mind, this chapter has perhaps been among the most complicated ones. We have brought the logic of science, philosophy, and religion, and tried to place them on the table. Although such a debate is usually only important when you study philosophy, this does not mean that in the West, such as in Christianity, such debates are any less important. In the Muslim world, it is very true that although they must make an effort to learn all these debates and argument, they themselves are not encouraged to take the debate any further, but rather to absorb it. After all, Muslims believe that with the compatibilism model, all the game in this subject is over. However, in Christianity, as discussed in other chapters, reason and mind were seen as important instruments towards knowing and drawing closer to The Almighty God. Therefore, the debate on such matters should always be bustling.

CHAPTER 9

Why Does God Allow Evil Things to Happen?

Introduction

I had an occasion where I was supervising a student on a topic concerning refugees. Out of left field, or I should say for a motive or reason unknown to me, the subject somehow completely changed when they asked me, in a rather aggressive tone the following question, "Why do evil things exist? Why does God allow such things to happen?" I tried to rationalise their questions, rather bewildered. I actually had many other points to discuss with them regarding the subject of refugees, and my mind at the time was thinking of something along the lines of "Migrating to another country is probably the best option for those who no longer can tolerate the problems or evil things occurring in their mother country." However, that thought was completely interrupted by the question which was suddenly thrown at me.

Why do evil things exist? Why does God allow such things to happen? Judging from their tone, I began to realise that these questions must have been guided by some sort of reason; not necessarily out of curiosity, but probably motivated by some kind of anger, maybe hatred, or other reasons. I also realised one other thing, the student is a Muslim, suggesting how outdated my perception about my fellow religionist or I should say how shallow my knowledge was about the younger generation among me. I have never encountered such questions while I am around fellow Muslims, especially thrown out with that kind of forceful tone. I do not exactly know why, but I responded to them by saying "These questions are about the Christian understanding of God". What I meant was these questions usually appear in discussions regarding God in Christianity. A moment later, I realised that I did not know much about Christianity, so I should not make such inference or judgement. However, I still asked myself why I wildly responded to the student's questions by referencing the Christian concept of God.

As I began to ponder my own response and kept searching for the answer, the term theodicy surfaced in one of the materials I gathered, and this became part of my inquiry.

In this chapter we will be discussing about:

1. What is Theodicy?

2. A Temporal Horror but with An Eternal Bliss

3. Existentialism

What is Theodicy?

To be honest, I have in fact encounter such problems with regard to the question of evil or bad things in this world, but I remember that my parents and *ustadh* immediately countered me by explaining that we are here in this world to be tested with good and bad things; if we choose to do good, we will be rewarded paradise, and vice versa. In those days, I pretty much just followed my parents and my *ustadh*'s conclusion on the matter. How about the bad or evil things that happen in this world that we do not choose such as flash flood or drought happening around our area, or the stories we hear of earthquakes, volcano eruptions, violence, war—the list continues.

We can probably call these said evil as moral evil and natural evil. These two categorisations are what I came across when I was embroiled in this subject of theodicy. Maybe I was right when I directed my thoughts to the idea of the Christian God as my student asked those questions. After all, based on the voluminous literature generated on this subject of evil, many of them revolve around the theological debates in Christianity. Although I know this topic called theology is present in Islam, I do not see it as ubiquitous as in Christian literature.

The word theodicy came from the Greek word *theos* which means god, and *dikē* which translates to justice. To put it in simpler terms, theodicy is the study of justifying god. You can frame the definition in any way which makes you most comfortable. When I say it is ubiquitous in Christian literature, I am trying to suggest it is something unique relative to other religions that I know in which in most cases they are not so deep of their discussion in this subject.

However, as I stumbled upon Christian theology, I came across with a belief quite opposite, which says that we carry the sins of Adam and Eve, therefore we have to be baptised (purified). I do not know whether the term I use here is correct. One thing that I am sure of though is that the discussion on theology or the attributes of God, as I have already informed earlier, is really extensive in Christianity from one side to the other side of the teaching. In other words, the subject of theology is a must if you are a Christian. Questions such as why evil things exist in the world and why God allows evil things to happen are questions that Christian theologians first began unpacking more than a thousand years ago, and they are still creatively trying to unpack it until today responding to the question of theodicy.

Why do evil things exist? Why does God allow such things to happen? These questions, as you are already aware, were forcefully asked to me by a fellow Muslim, and in reaction to this event, I began to rationalise the background of this person. I have in fact encountered many other questions from others which I never thought would be uttered by them. For example, statements or question like these have befall upon me:

"Why must we have God who wants His creations to worship and praise Him?"

"Why must I be responsible for my sins when He has predetermined whether I will follow His order or not?"

"There are thousands of Gods. If I really have to believe in one, can I not choose?"

I sat back and scratched my head, contemplating on those questions. I did ask some of my colleagues to perhaps shine some light upon these questions, and in response to my request, some of them (some are experts on Islamic studies) said that before they reply to my question regarding my student's inquiry, I should answer a question from them first. They asked me "Why did they ask those questions to you, and not to us?" While I am aware of the logic behind my colleagues' question, that is a separate issue which is beyond the scope of this chapter, but the short answer to it is not only do I have strong interest in philosophy, I also taught a subject which was closely related to philosophy.

When I checked back on the background of those who would usually ask me these kinds of questions, a few selected characteristics are rather noticeable among them. Firstly, they are English educated. Secondly, they are very vocal. Thirdly, they believe in the power of argument with some sense of entitlement. These qualities are worthy to be emulated. In fact, such qualities are required nowadays. Perhaps it is not an exaggeration for me to say that the information they gathered on religion are mostly from English references, and discussions on religion in the West are centred on the teachings of Christianity, thus I can also say that the theological questions they placed on the table are questions of philosophy in response to Christianity in the West. Now, I can rationalise a little more why I mentioned the Christian God when they asked me the question on theodicy. What essentially is the Christian God seeing that the three religions came from the same source, the Abrahamic faith? This is just a question out of my curiosity.

There are many books which discuss the subject of theodicy, and out of these works, John Hick is well known for his work regarding this topic. I came to know that, at least by the early accounts of those with authority in Christianity such as Saint Augustine, such a concept of God in Christianity began with the idea of the Original Sin and the concept of The Fall. According to this idea, God created a perfect world, and the first of mankind Adam and Eve, as well as the angels were given the choice to do whatever they want as long as they follow God's commandments. At least this is the way that I understand it. When Adam and Eve ate the forbidden fruit which was against God's commandments, they committed a sin and were thrown onto earth, hence the origin of The Fall as well as the Original Sin.

Subsequently, with God's mercy or benevolence, Jesus (the god on earth) was sent down onto this earth to save mankind from the suffering of evil things which happen because of the Original Sin. Jesus sacrificed himself for mankind, thus whosoever follows Jesus, according to this belief, will be saved by the evil and enter paradise (salvation). Evil things in this world happen because of the bad things people commit as they carry their sin, and because they refuse to do good things as Jesus told them to. I do not want to pretend like I do know a lot about this subject, but at least we know a little bit of something on why evil and bad things happen in this world from this account. Moral evils such as robbery, killing, and war happen because of the Original Sin, and natural evils such as earthquakes and volcanic eruptions happen because people still continue to do bad things.

I should probably mention here how questions of philosophy or religiophilosophy become quite ubiquitous in Christianity in comparison to Islam. St. Augustine who embroiled himself with the Bible scripture also engrossed himself with Plato's philosophy. Those of you who may have heard of the theory of forms and ideas which was theorised or rather philosophised by Plato may have also heard how for instance the chair that we see every day is just the idea of the chair. The real chair, as Plato said, exists in the metaphysical world.

St. Augustine coined the term *privatio boni* or the absence of goodness in explaining the idea of evil. Simplifying massively, there is nothing in this world that should be understood as evil. What actually is happening is called the absence of goodness. I do not think the student who asked me those questions could easily swallow Augustine's explanation, and neither can I. The question of why God allows evil things to happen is probably just inherently problematic itself.

To analogise the concept of *privatio boni*, perhaps we can try and compare it with the problems with our smartphones. We should not understand the phone as a bad appliance, but rather a non-good appliance, or to put it more appropriately in accordance with the principle of *privatio boni*, the absence of goodness in the smartphone. This argument follows the legacy of Plato and his followers, including Augustine. This approach was later called Neoplatonism. By the way, Neoplatonism is also widespread in the Muslim World. God, according to this belief, is so good, and with His All-Goodness, it is impossible that evil could come from Him.

Maybe at this juncture I should also say something on eschatology. Speaking of which, just a side joke, when I first mentioned this term to a few colleagues of mine and tried to survey in case they already know of this concept, one of them jokingly or perhaps honestly (since she is known for her many virtuous characters) said, "I do know the meaning of *loji* (sewage plant), but I am not aware of the term 'eschatol', although I do know of the term *ais ketul* (ice cube)". With such a terrible joke, maybe it is advisable for me to cover my face immediately.

Jokes aside, eschatology is the study or the science of giving rationality to the idea of the End of Time, in which it is said in Christianity that Jesus would come to save mankind. Christians believe that through the famous event of Crucifixion, at least two important things occurred. First, Jesus willingly sacrificed himself for mankind, or I should say for the Christians to prevent them from continuing to suffer from the sin committed by Adam and Eve. Second, since the evil of the sin is too huge, only a human with God's essence can save mankind.

Of course, there is a lot of criticism with regard to Augustine's theodicy theory, and this should be expected. However, I have to say that the use of reason or philosophy in Christianity today is really out of my religious understanding. After all, in Islam, such employment of philosophy is very limited.

To proceed further, let us now turn to my suggestion and some of what the authoritative figures say on what we can understand about theodicy in the context of Islam.

A Temporal Horror but with An Eternal Bliss

Well, I feel awkward to talk about the idea of theodicy in Islam. The idea justifies that evil things happen in this world despite the existence of The All Benevolent God. After all, I have never thought of such matters except only recently. I must admit, part of the problem is myself, failing to recognise that such problems could also be rampant in my religion.

However, I still would like to respond to the question of theodicy, at least the way I myself understand it from my readings and from YouTube discussions which I follow, such as the video titled *Theodicy, God and Suffering—A debate between Dinesh D'Souza and Bart Ehrman.* Hence, the following ideas must be taken with a pinch of salt and should be understood as coming from a non-expert.

Firstly, we happen to understand that tigers do brutally kill their prey. However, even the word "brutally" is just a word applied from human morality imposed on nature. Can we say that evil took place? Can we also say that it is part of

God's act? I do not think so, but you are right, because tigers have no principle of choice or free-will, implying that what it does is just done naturally without any moral law attached to it. But, when we know that Hitler killed six million Jews during the Holocaust, can we call such an atrocity an evil act? I do think we can, and of course I believe that it is an atrocity. However, why should we blame God when Hitler can exercise choice, to kill or not to kill, unlike the tiger? Why must we blame God but not blame Hitler?

Secondly, I feel really awkward now because what is placed on the table, the question of Godhood, which I am aware that human beings are just His creations, and as a slave, what position do I have to question the existence of God or His Godhood? After all, if we believe (which I do) that He is omnipotent and omniscient, what right do I have, or why should I feel entitled to question His Might? I was told when I was a kid that we as kids do not know why our parents decide the way they decide, but we do know that when our mum is angry at us, even pinching us, we never blamed her for doing evil acts on us. Obviously, God is beyond such trivial examples. Hence, I would like to move to the third point.

Thirdly, there is a principle in Islam called *tanzikh* or Divine Transcendence and *tashbih* or Divine Immanence, the former speaks about the metaphysical law, while the latter on moral or religious law. Just put aside these probably mumbo-jumbo concepts to those who are new to this idea. But, I would like to give a scenario which I listened from a debate on YouTube on this subject of theodicy. If you happen to see a car in a car park with one of its doors open, with two babies wailing inside, it would probably be natural for us to make the judgment of "Where is their parent or guardian? How could someone do such an evil thing?". We are so quick to judge things that happen in front of us, and this is normal. Perhaps, once we know that their mother had just heard that their father had a heart attack, and kind of lost her mind rushing to get to her husband, then our judgment on such evilness changes. I remember reading Steven Covey's book, in which on one occasion, a man reading a newspaper became anxious when there were children who were moving about in every direction without control while their father was there. This might suggest that the father is a bad parent. The man talked to the father, "Can you control your kids? They are disturbing the others." The man replied with "Oh sorry, their mother just passed away, I just could not control myself".

The point that I am making here is that we do not have enough information in this world. How can we feel ourselves as larger than this planet, questioning the power and benevolence of God? This is the point when I start with the idea of Divine Transcendence, in which there are things which are beyond our comprehension, beyond our abilities to conceive and perceive. At this point, I suddenly remember the theory of *kasb* (acquisition) in Islam, it has bearings with the idea of theodicy. I will try to have this thing settled in the next chapter (God-willing).

Fourthly, recall my student who posed the question of "Why evil happens and why God allows it to happen?" The following discussion of course must be read with the earlier three points. I think when people talk about God, most of them are talking about the idea of God, not The God. No one can comprehend God, but only the idea. People disagree with the idea, nothing with regards to God. In Islam, everything is a creation or ideas on creation. But there is one thing that the Muslims strongly believe, and that is God, or I should carefully say, the speech of God, which is the Quran.

Muslims believe that there is no other way people can know of God except by reading or understanding what God says or reveals about Himself. I was told that we were told in the Quran about the names and attributes of God. According to Quranic sources, there are at least 99 names of God, and interestingly, there are names that reflect benignity, such as *Jamal* (Beauty) and there is also the name *Jalal* (Majestic). My reading revealed to me that God is aware of all aspects of His creation, including, most crucially, people's perceptions of good and evil based on those names. Probably, because we Muslims do not have much knowledge on the Quran, after all, not everyone was given such knowledge by The Almighty God to comprehend it. Of course, He is All-Knowing, He knows what He is doing. If God is also The Avenger (*Muttaqin*), Majestic (*Jalal*), and The King (*Malik*), it does not imply the dimension of the All-Goodness and All-Loving to which we understand. Perhaps, since we do not understand the true meaning of All-Goodness to us, then we take it that everything that seems evil to us is also evil to The Almighty God. This is counter-intuitive for the simple reason that we will know later on God's attribute then what God says in The Quran.

I should probably end this section by repeating what I have said earlier, that everything that happens in this world has happened because The Almighty God wanted it to happen. Every cloud has a silver lining. In Islam, there is a concept of test. We are here in this world and tested by both good things and bad things the way we understand them. But, I think that we would only bring the same problem if we begin to ask, "Why must God test us, if He is All-Knowing and knows of the outcome of the tests?" I think that such questions only invite the problem of secularity. Muslims are taught to be humble in front of God. Even this world might seem evil, such as natural disasters, earthquake, volcanoes, thunderstorm, or pandemics such as COVID-19, Muslims and those in other religions to learn that there is an eternal bliss for those who are afflicted by those horrors, or I should say they died as martyrs and are promised with paradise. If we are really humble and want to understand how compassionate God is, whatever evil lies in this world is just only temporary, and eternal bliss awaits those who are in the position of admitting their slavehood, unlike those who are Godless, with ego larger than the universe.

I would like to end this section by saying what normally Muslims say, or I should say good Muslims say, when they end their speech, which goes as follows. Everything that is good and virtuous in what I have said comes from The Almighty God, and everything bad and evil comes from my own weakness. May God bless us. We will discuss about existentialism in the next part—on the question of whether we really have the freedom of choice. Although it has no direct bearing to the idea of theodicy, I think we should try and understand this subject of existentialism because the founders of this idea rejected the idea of God and to a certain extent also rejected the idea of philosophy and ended up believing on human feelings only. This is controversial integrally, especially for the younger generations since radical individual choice seems to have become their new norm, and this norm is detrimental to those with religious beliefs.

Existentialism

It has become a part of me that nearly every time I begin my discussion, I would start by throwing some riddles. I remember on a few occasions, when I asked my audience the following question: if you happen to come upon a ring which would grant you invisibility when you wear it, what would you do with it? While this is not originally mine and has been used ever since the Greeks, of course modified to suit modern situations. I received various feedback, and interestingly, some tried to read into my mind instead of reading into the riddle. Some of them said "I think I know you want us to say that if we cannot be seen by others, we will tend to do evil things". Sure enough, they got me wrong. I really just wanted to know what their answers would be. Others would say that they would not do any bad thing regardless of whether they can or cannot be seen by others.

I think I do know, more or less, that this person just wants to prove me wrong. The implicit message in the riddle is that when people have the opportunity to not be seen by others, they will tend to do evil things. This tells us the basic idea of human nature. Actually, I did press further by handing out follow-up questions to them, asking them that if they think for a moment, what actually is stopping them from doing evil things. They immediately reprimanded me and said that no, they would never do bad things even in such a circumstance.

I believe there is something missing in this exercise, including what is implicit in the riddle. Should we not say that yes, we are invisible to others, but we are not invisible to The Almighty God? The aspect of being visible to The Almighty God is not there in nearly every discussion that I follow in the West. However, there are discussions that may be useful for us to relate with this riddle. Have you ever encountered a quotation such as the following?

For an authentic existence, one should act as oneself, not as "one's acts" or as "one's genes" or any other essence.

This quotation explains the idea of existentialism.

The idea in the quotation suggests the idea of ourselves as the author or the king of our own decisions. We should not make decisions based on our acts because our acts have already been contaminated by others' ideas, such as that of parents, religion, ideology, and the like. This is what the existentialists want us to do. We should not even act by following our genes or gender, implying that whether we are black or white, male or female, these are the categories which should not stop us from making choices when it comes to doing, being, and feeling what we want.

The aspects of our genes, gender, and everything else which is defined by others, the so-called experts, are called essentials. Were we born with those essentials, or did we come into existence into this world like a blank slate? Traditionally, we understand ourselves, as we were born, as having these essentials or identity, both biologically and even ethnically. It is just like water. The essential of water is H2O, and the same applies to human beings. According to the existentialists, while this concept may apply to things and animals, it does not necessarily apply to human beings due to the fact that humans can make choices—the choices to do, to be, and to feel what they want to. Therefore, humans have to be the masters of choices to make them truly human, hence the idea of individual choice: veto power to individuals.

You may want to know who the important figures are behind this philosophy and movement of a sort. Notable amongst them are Søren Kierkegaard, Jean-Paul Sartre, Simone de Beauvoir, Albert Camus, and many others.

My question is why, in the state of *tabula rasa*, we cannot hold the idea of God, meaning that we are completely blank except the idea of soul? This may be complicated to some of you, but it brings us back to the riddle earlier. If you are invisible to others, then you would hypothetically be in your state of nature. We will tend to do evil things, but if in our state of nature, we do have the idea of God in mind, then we are not exactly invisible.

Probably, to get the current generation to understand easier, what are we by default, or in our factory state? In my religion, all of us, and I mean all human beings, are equally blessed with souls, the entities blown into us by angels, the agents of God. The soul will not die when we die. It lives eternally. Thus, we actually will never die if we awaken our soul. In fact, if all of us repent or ask for The Almighty's forgiveness, all of us would enter paradise. I guess one cannot understand existentialism, either its contents or substance, without first reviewing Nietzsche's idea, which is generally understood as nihilism.

To say something on nihilism, we must understand that Nietzsche not only rejected the idea of religion, but also philosophy. For him, this is just stupidity or two sides of the same coin. Throwing religion would mean throwing philosophy, and vice versa. To him, morality itself is just a relativity.

Nietzsche once said that God is dead, what he meant was that humans have already rejected religion and are in hopes for philosophy. But life is so empty when we have rejected religion, which according to him is nonsensical, the philosophy that people are hopeful of is just another nonsense. This is nihilism.

I don't think that you have ever come across the terms absurd facticity, authenticity, angst, and the looks of others. According to existentialists, the facts of our life are not our own facts. It is the facts imagined by religious people. It is really absurd because with them we cannot live with our own selves but with absurd facticity. Hence, to live life with authenticity, we have to live a life where we choose what we want to do, be, and feel, and do so in the way we want to. We are by default depressed beings (angsty). The only way that we can be happy is not to do what other people say but to follow our own selves. Finally, it is of course not easy to follow what we want in the presence of others' looks. Yes, existentialists may say we need time and we cannot run from the absurd facticity in one day or even one week. They further claim that as we try more and more, perhaps next month or next year, we can live our very own authentic life.

I think I should not leave you without giving my comments. Firstly, with this belief, the idea of giving veto to people to make choices the way we want, would make the world look ugly. People used to follow religions, and after that philosophy, and now, according to existentialists, just feelings.

Secondly, the longing towards doing good things is a natural thing (*fitrah*) and our primordial nature, and we definitely do need guidance to understand and practise the good things in life. We also need religion or philosophy, and there are facts that tell us those with religion and philosophy live happier lives than those who follow their feelings. Lastly, existentialists have something to say on the potential for committing suicide because of angst, the default state of anxiety or depression. "The ultimate hero of absurdism lives without meaning and faces suicide without succumbing to it." This saying to me at best only leaves people in a state of limbo.

Conclusion

I really hope this chapter has helped you and I understand clearer on the questions of theodicy, as well as existentialism. From my experience in discussing about philosophy during my classes, I notice that many of the young generations have been unknowingly influenced by the dogma of existentialism, and it is not a strange thing that the word 'choice' seems to become their mantra in every opportunity they have when discussing about the idea of philosophy.

As I ponder on the subject of radical individual choice, there is a voice which asks me "Why don't you write a book on *Does Choice Really Exist?*". Maybe I'll give it some thought.

CHAPTER 10

Conclusion:
Does Islam Have
a Philosophy?

Introduction

Quite relatively recently, I've been busy planning to move to a place that is more conducive for me to work on issues concerning religion, philosophy, and politics. I was summoned by my senior to explain this plan of mine to transfer to a new place. As I was explaining how I wanted to focus on Islam and philosophy through the phone, out of the blue he asked me the following question: "Does Islam have a philosophy?"

I was quite puzzled as I sat back and wondered how I should respond to this instance. The question had me stuck between a rock and a hard place. Was this really a question, or rather just a statement? If it really was a question, which I believe it was, was this question asked out of curiosity? I do know my senior very well. After all, we've been working at the same place for more than two whole decades.

To many people, including Muslims, be it back in those days or even today, the world of philosophy is not necessarily looked at with gleaming eyes, but it is also not seen with appalling and disdaining eyes either. By the way, this is the idea that I wanted to share, that which I understood as philosophy, although most of the people that I do know do not see debates on God's existence as a philosophical matter, but rather part of the discussion of systematic theology.

In this concluding chapter, I would like to spend my time grappling with this question. Does Islam have a philosophy? To be more precise, do Muslims teach and learn philosophy?

Notes: A large chunk of the discussions in this section are derived from Timothy Winter's explanation on theology and mysticism in Islam, as can be found in his YouTube uploads.

In this chapter we will be discussing about:

1.   Philosophy in Islam and its Counterargument

2.   Theomorphism in Philosophical Islam

3.   The Concentric Model of Islam

Philosophy in Islam and Its Counterargument

I realised that there are literature which strongly suggest that Islam has no teaching on the aspect of reason, therefore there is no way Islam can foster philosophy.

Islam was not understood as a religion of orthodoxy, instead a religion of orthopraxy. The former indicates the debate of the existence of God, implying the idea of philosophy, while the latter suggests the concept of spiritual practices, such as worship and fasting, implying the legalistic or jurisprudential nature. When I mentioned orthodoxy and orthopraxy, one of my colleagues felt like avoiding reading this chapter. I sensed that they wanted terms that are indigenously Islamic to be used instead. Hence, to make it more convenient and readable, I think it would be better to use vocabularies or categories indigenous to Muslims, which are *aqidah* or theology in Islam for orthodoxy, and *ibadah* (or spiritualistic aspects of worship) for orthopraxy.

There are several books on this subject of Islam and philosophy which I know of, such as that which was written by Majid Fakhry which I commonly refer to, another by Seyyed Hossein Nasr. Although I do not know much about thinkers in my country who are really into this line of study, I do know that some of them are in fact students or followers of these thinkers. In early Islam, sometimes called the first three generations of Islam, there is no such thing as philosophy, and nothing that can even be called as systematic theology. The influx of Greek thinkers' ideas such as those of Plato and Aristotle shook the very basic ideas of Islam.

It should be noted that although neither philosophy nor systematic theology existed, it does not mean that the Quran did not talk about the question of mind as a way in understanding God. In fact, there is a hadith known as the Hadith of Jibril (Gabriel) which distinctly states that the three spheres of humanhood (of which I will explain with the concentric model towards the end of this chapter) concurrently exist. In case you are curious on what this Hadith of Jibril is, you can just search it up on Google or any other search engines. I'm certain it will show up. What I'm trying to say here is that there is no systematic discussion or inquiry on the subject of theology and philosophy at the time because everyone saw the behaviours of Prophet Muhammad SAW and his companions and pretty much worked towards following their footsteps.

The giant philosophers in Islam, including Al-Farabi and Ibn Sina who quite almost literally favour reason, have been more than celebrated in the West. The fact that they are celebrated in the Western world tells us something about the different teachings of religion in the Muslim world, besides the aspect of *ibadah* (worship) mentioned earlier. In the Islamic world, at least the way I understand it, the discussion on the attributes and nature of God (theology) is of course indifferently an important subject, especially if we were to look at the discussion on the "20 Attributes of The Almighty God", one of the common approaches within the Sunni group when it comes to dealing with the question of God. However, the real question is whether you are a theologian who is scripture-sensitive or mind-sensitive. In different words, are you a person of the Revelation or a person who heavily relies on reason?

Invariably, in order to become better and more

balanced, a Muslim should embrace both revelation and reason. My point here is that if the arguments collide, which should you give priority to? The two giant Muslim philosophers I mentioned earlier literally gave privilege to reason over revelation, hence why they are perhaps more celebrated, and their ideas taken more easily in the West. By the way, there are three other philosophers who are similarly great and needs to be mentioned here: Ibn Bajjah, Ibn Tufayl, and Ibn Rushd, and the latest produced voluminous works on philosophical Islam which are referred to even today. In fact, there is a school of thought called Averroism which popularised Ibn Rushd's paradigm of Double Truth, in which its philosophy and theology are taught in the West. Averroism is, of course, a school of thought taken from the name of Ibn Rushd (Averroes). He was not only a philosopher, but also a Maliki jurist in Cordoba.

Regarding philosophy in Islam, you may be surprised if I were to say that there are some in Islam who believe that Islam has no philosophy and is only about the worship component. In the following section, we will further discuss this.

Well, the fact that there are arguments established rejecting the idea of philosophy in Islam owes a lot of explanation. Importantly, why must Islam reject philosophy, and what is the status of the five aforementioned philosophers and people with similar standings when it comes to this?

In my mind, those who support the rejection of philosophy usually bring up this question: "What is the value of Islam with the Quran and hadith at its centre if just by Plato and Aristotle's philosophies can help Muslims understand the truth of God?" To put the question differently, "Who would Muslims want to follow: Prophet Muhammad and his sahabah whose core teaching is based on the revelation, or Plato and Aristotle whose idea is based on reason?"

It is probably worth to mention a few names of those who did not subscribe to the idea of philosophy in Islam. Names such as Ibn Qudamah al-Maqdisi and his ideas can be traced back to Ahmad Ibn Hanbal, hence can be traced back to the sahabah and the Prophet. Ibn Qudamah himself has a book titled *Censure of Speculative Theology*, a book which explains how wicked and blasphemous those who rely only on reason are.

My hunch tells me that many Western researchers have probably read this book, hence it is not strange if some of them argue that Islam has no teaching which applies reason, or to put it bluntly, Islam has no philosophy at all.

The followers of Ibn Qudamah's approach are sometimes grouped under the name of "Literalist Muslims" for their heavy emphasis or sensitivity to the revelation and hadith statements. Their followers are just as many as those who did not follow this group. On the other hand, the opposite of this group—those who heavily give emphasis on logic and reason are known as "Rationalist Muslims", and a lot of Muslim philosophers belong to this group.

I should mention that in my family's setting, the majority of the older generation gravitate towards being literalists. There was an occasion in which they asked me what it was that I teach at the university. I replied with, "*I teach political philosophy*", which I now have re-termed as political thought. As I had expected, although they tried to maintain their cool, I could sense from their voice a tone which hinted at head scratching and eyebrow raising the moment I uttered the word "philosophy". But of course, I understand where my family came from, and all of them are good people— that is what's more important to me.

I do not regard myself as belonging to the group of rationalists, but rather subscribing to the literalist meaning in a different way. To be honest, even until today, I still can't figure out how there are philosophers in the Muslim world, at least for the past nine to ten centuries, who argue something like the following:

Of course, the revelations were descended to the Prophet by Jibril. However, we must understand that the people who were the immediate targets of these revelations were the less intellectually gifted desert dwellers. Hence, they needed simple stories for their level of mind, to make them understand the ideas of the Absolute Truth. If the Quran is already there to explain everything, why does God then insist us to use our reasoning?"

These so-called philosophers further highlighted that if those who used their reason such as Plato and Aristotle managed to understand reality and even find out that there is God by using their reasoning, hence we should have a choice either to understand the Absolute Truth by following the narrations in the Quran and hadith or by following the philosophical path. I myself scratched my head and raised my eyebrows when reading materials which make such arguments. I do not think that I can reason out what is in the mind of those philosophers, even if I were to be given another life to try and make sense of them. I hope that I say this out of humility and humbleness and not in hatred against the philosophers.

In the next part, I will try to succinctly discuss the main debate on philosophical Islam.

Theomorphism in Philosophical Islam

I'm well aware that I'm about to encounter huge difficulties in explaining the concept of theomorphism, and with it, anthropomorphism. Theomorphism, crudely put, is the idea that divine presence exists in us, while anthropomorphism on the other hand is the debate that God carries human attributes, saying that God has hands, eyes, like how humans do. Mormonism flourishes as an absolute example of religious anthropomorphism.

Let's glance back to the dialogue between my senior and I which was mentioned at the beginning of this chapter, when they asked me directly, "Does Islam have a philosophy?". This particular section of the chapter is where I would like to explain whatever I know on the topic, arguing yes, it does. We are going to discuss a few concepts or doctrines in Islam and end by landing on Al-Ghazali's synthesis of "God created man in His image". If you feel uncomfortable with this phrase (which is clearly theomorphic) and this subject, you can skip this section and jump onto the next. The reason I say so is because when I first heard of this idea around thirty years ago, I too felt uncomfortable about it.

To begin with, there are many hadith in Islam from which

this phrase may have been derived from, including by the towering figures when it comes to the compilation of ethical sayings of Prophet Muhammad SAW, such as al-Bukhari and Muslim. Muslim narrated that Abu Hurayrah said:

The Messenger of Allah (peace and blessings of Allah be upon him) said: "When any one of you fights his brother, let him avoid the face, for Allah created Adam in His image." (Sahih Muslim, Hadith 2612)

Interestingly, such an idea had also developed in the Christian world, but this is not strange at all because the phrase is also present in the Bible. For instance, in Genesis 1:27, it is mentioned:

"So God created man in His own image, in the image of God He created him; male and female He created them."

What is the thesis or first premise of this so-called philosophy of theomorphism? Some Muslims may know about the story of the three brothers told in classical Islam, and we would like to use this story in our discussion, thus here we go.

Of the three brothers, one of them was kind, another was wicked, and the third died as a child, so the first is in paradise, the second in hell and the third is in a limbo where he experiences neither reward nor punishment. Thus, the third in the next life explains to God that he was never given the chance to obey God, hence unable to be rewarded paradise. Therefore, he complains to God for having him die before he even had the chance to work towards heaven. On the other hand, the second brother speaks up and asks why had he not been made to die young as well? If that was the case, he would have been spared hell as well.

What is the philosophy behind this story? If God must be consistent as the idea of free-will among the group called Mu'tazilah insists, what is the philosophical argument that the free-will can offer for the second brother to die and enter paradise? It is God's decision to choose who dies first, who dies second and who enters hellfire.

This is among the variants of antitheses put forward by the compatibilists, of which many of them are currently grouped under the banner of Asha'irah. In Islam, it is not our good acts that guarantee whether or not we merit paradise, but rather it is through His mercy and compassion that people will be punished and rewarded. Therefore, it is wrong to impose our own principle of moral consistency on God.

Predestinarians or Mujbirah on the other hand believe that we have no free-will whatsoever from the very beginning of our creation to the way we live in this world, and even to the moment we are sent to paradise or hellfire. Predestinarians almost literally believe that we human beings are placed on autopilot and are set for either one of the two targets: paradise or hellfire.

By the way, since I have mentioned the topic of anthropomorphism, which is the belief in God having eyes or hands or any physical characteristics like us humans, I better share here the little bit that I know on this subject based on Yasir Qadhi's postulation. Questions regarding such topic have glancingly appeared even during the time of the first three generations of Islam. The simple response for such questions was: "The meaning is explicitly clear, asking it is *bid'ah* (innovation)", which means that no one during Prophet Muhammad SAW's time and the first three generations had ever asked or explained this question in detail. However, as Yasir Qadhi once said, this sort of questions must be dealt with in our generation because Muslims no longer live during the glorious times.

The fact is that such phrases do exist in the Quran, and that all Muslims must believe in it. But the problem is that some Muslims try to imagine and interpret the description in those phrases in the form of how we humans understand it. We imagine the "hand" and "eyes" mentioned in the verses of the Quran as hands and eyes the way we humans see it in this world. We interpret "anger" and "laugh" the way we get angry and laugh. That is our problem, and it is our own issue to fix. If the Quran says that in paradise, there is a "cup", of course the fact that there is a cup in paradise cannot be denied, but the Quran also makes it clear as to not imagine how the cup looks like or what it is made out of, because we are unable to. Yasir Qadhi insisted that Muslims must believe that there is a cup in paradise, and that God has eyes and hands the way that God explains it in the Quran—but that should literally be the only way they try to understand it; never should they try to imagine it with the limited human brain.

With that said, we shall now focus back on the idea of theomorphism. Before we reach the idea of "God created man in His image", there are two other doctrines, or at least I should say two doctrines left to discuss. The first is on moral neutrality, and the second is on *kasb* (acquisition). These are again some of the variants of the antitheses introduced by the compatibilists.

The idea of moral neutrality is championed by Muhammad al-Shahrastani who wrote a lot of influential books, in which many are translated into English, if you are interested. Like many other contemporary philosophers, he invited us to respond to his hypothetical case, and the story of the three brothers earlier was also a hypothetical case.

Have you ever wondered why do I say that philosophy does indeed exist in the Muslim world? Many of the debates put forward by philosophers are indeed hypothetical questions. In order to convey his moral neutrality on God, he told us to imagine a fully competent person whose knowledge on morality, ethics, God, and the concept of evil have not been taught or even been close to his mind, being thrown into a deserted island. He is able to comprehend all other forms of knowledge: biology, chemistry, physics, and many others. However, were he to one day witness a murder happening in front of him, he would not be able to rationalise that such an act of evil took place in front of him.

The following doctrine of acquisition or *kasb* further explains how philosophy or systematic theology is very important in the Muslim world. Simplifying massively, this doctrine entails the logic and belief that all actions, good and evil, originate from God, but they are acquired by men. Subsequent compatibilists emerging after the introduction of this doctrine continued advocating this philosophy of *kasb*. Of course, logical questions are naturally expected when discussing such a topic, so let us have a look at one of them. How can God apparently judge people for their wrongdoing, when He Himself is The Omnipotent Creator of all actions?

Try to distinguish between God's creation of acts on one hand and a person's acquisition of acts on the other. Now, try to understand how humans cannot act without the acts of God. What I want you to consider is to think that we can choose any act, but it must simultaneously align with the act of God. The doctrine claims that punishment is also a consequence of our choice, hence compatibilists believe that there is a kind of instantaneous bubble that encloses the acts of humans and the acts of God, or at least that is how Timothy Winter called it. Without a doubt, the doctrine of *kasb* carries or invites some elements of mysticism.

Now, we turn to the synthesis of this saga by directing our attention to the great Muslim philosopher of the past to enlighten us on this unquestionably puzzling concept, and who else would the philosopher be if not Al-Ghazali. He solved every piece of the puzzle by stating that moral decisions are located in the conscience, and that the self-aware core of the human creature is not located in the mind but the soul. Mark you, to me, this theomorphic remark is a very strong statement because if it is no longer at the level of the mind, then it implies that no philosophy is needed, period.

Man is created to be God's deputy on Earth. Pretty much every Muslim knows this injunction very well. When man truly becomes His deputy or *khalifah*, implying they really concentrate their body, mind, and soul to The Almighty when performing worship, we will see that the separation of a man's will from the will of God only exists in our mind, and that it is merely an illusion. When this occurs, some sort of mystical experience takes place where the light of God touches the human light (light upon light), and this requires us to understand the science of unveiling, of which I don't have any clue nor authority to continue discussing about.

However, Timothy Winter did mention that what it means is that humans as theomorphic beings partake in all of the divine attributes in a contingent way, including *qudrah* (the attribute of will). God is The Most Compassionate, and human beings can be compassionate as well, obviously in a contingent manner. As God is The Most Just, and human beings also are just as well. This is how the Ghazalian thinking provided a solution to this paradox of good and evil in this world. This is the explanation of "God created man in His image", the synthesis I brought up earlier.

The Concentric Model of Islam

In this part, I will try to explain how the Hadith of Jibril which details on the three spheres can be demonstrated by understanding the concentric model of Islam as in the diagram below. By the way, have you searched the internet for the hadith?

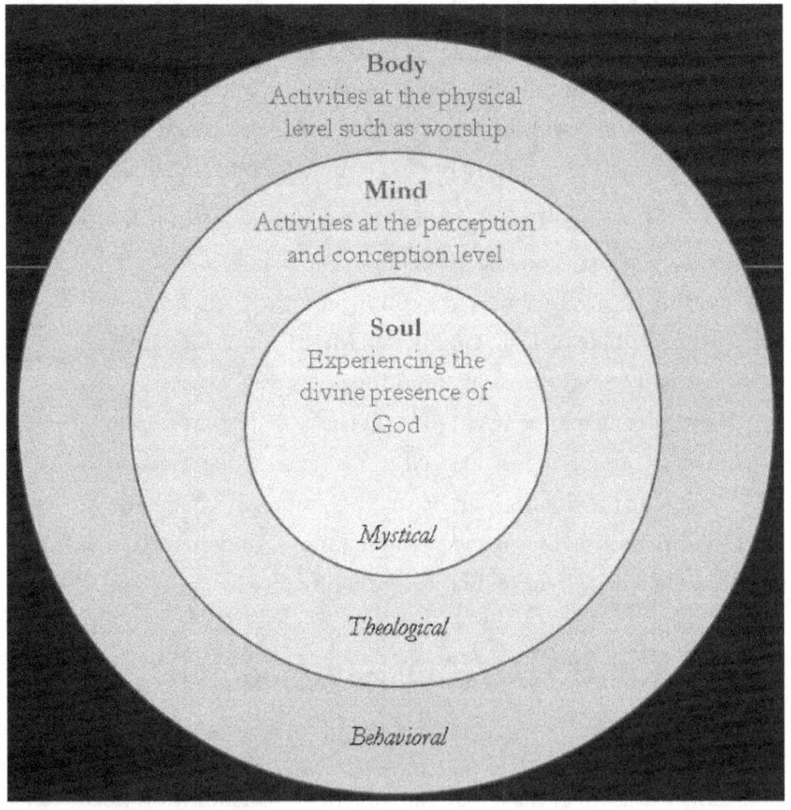

Let us begin by noting that the area outside of the biggest circle in the diagram is mankind, and as you make the confession to be a Muslim, you are already entering the biggest circle.

In the Muslim scheme of thinking, this is the realm of *ibadah* or orthopraxy mentioned earlier, referring to the Five Pillars of Islam: testimony or declaration of faith (*shahadah*), prayer, fasting, almsgiving, and pilgrimage (*hajj*).

Every pillar after the confession are activities which require actions or behaviours at the body level. It does not matter if the individual is still immoral, as we probably know that there are many immoral Muslims, but as long as they make the confession "There is no God but Him, and Prophet Muhammad is the final Messenger of God", whether or not they perform the act of *ibadah* does not really matter. What really matters is that they make the attempt to practise it or at the very least, as a beginner they must learn how to practise, and they are still considered Muslims. It is of course an obligation for them to work towards the utmost spiritual level of *ibadah*. In fact, there are potential punishments for those who ignore it. Their acts of *ibadah* are rewarded not with the act in itself but by the Compassion and Mercy of The Almighty God.

Do understand that it does not mean that the acts of worship do not matter. Everyone is equal in the "eye" of God as indicated earlier, because all of us mankind, whether we are outside of the biggest circle or inside it, are blessed with the blessings of the soul. However, we are also not equal because not everyone is blessed with a good ability to reason out things like philosophers. Hence, Muslims would be in great advantage if they have a better understanding of the logic or reason as to why they perform these acts of orthopraxy together with the declaration of faith. This implies that if you have the knowledge on why God tells you to pray and fast, then you can perform them with more confidence. Those who do not have the ability to understand are required to make an attempt or effort to understand the knowledge, stimulating their thoughts and mind to understand God's commands, and even God's True Self.

These are the activities in the sphere of the smaller circle, a circle of thought in which Muslims develop our theological and philosophical knowledge. Muslims are taught the six principles of *iman* (faith): Belief in The Almighty God, the angels, the prophets, the books, the Day of Judgement, and the concept of doom and divine decree (*Qadha'* and *Qadr*). Muslims are required to understand each and every one of them.

The main takeaway is that within the philosophy of free-will, as we indicated in the section earlier, the activity of philosophical discourse takes place in the realm of theology displayed in the diagram. Again, it is not knowledge that guarantees whether a person can draw closer to God. It does help, of course, but it is through the Compassion and Mercy of God that they may do so.

Okay, so what is left to discuss now? Yes, you're right, the realm that is at the centre of the circle—the mystical realm. For this realm I would like to bring your attention towards the story of Iblis or Satan's refusal to bow down to Adam which is very well known in Islam. It is true that Adam was made nearly entirely from clay, but it is the soul which was blown by The Almighty God into him that made Adam and mankind what they are. It is a status which even the angels and all the habitants of heaven must bow down too.

It is commonly understood that through the process of purifying oneself (*tazkiyyah*), one can be called into this realm of mystical mystery. This process of soul purification is sometimes taught under the name of *Tasawwuf* or spiritual *ihsan*. We should not immediately attempt to understand *Tasawwuf* and Sufism, as the subject of Sufism requires separate treatment.

If you happen to read the Hadith of Jibril which also describes the components of *ihsan*, you will come across the following saying from the Prophet:

"… That you worship Allah as if you are seeing Him, for though you don't see Him, He, verily, sees you."

Well, I guess it is only this much that I can say about this realm. Why so? This realm is not the realm of thought, the realm of thought lies in the second circle. Beyond this circle is the realm of experience, in which one has to purify themselves in order to experience the divine presence. I better not pretend like I know much about this, because I was told that it is not expressible in human language and vocabulary. We are both in the dark on this one. It is beyond what can be conceived, and beyond what can be perceived.

Then, what exactly is it? That, I do not know. With that said, I think I better quickly conclude this chapter.

Conclusion

We began this chapter by sharing my story and knowledge pertaining to the question of "Does Islam have a philosophy?" and ended this chapter by orchestrating a discussion on the so-called concentric model of Islam; the three circles which relates to the idea of behavioural, theological and mystical Islam. In between these chapters, we discussed three important subjects which are what philosophy is in Islam, why there are rejections of philosophy in Islam, and the theomorphic aspects of Islam.

When I write this chapter and this book in its whole, my target audience encompasses everyone, regardless of whether you are a Muslim or belonging to other religions. I must say that this is a very ambitious project, and I was told that an ambitious man is a very dangerous man. If there is in fact something dangerous or precarious in this project, I believe it must have stemmed from my arrogance and ego. Therefore, I pray to the Almighty God to pardon me. And if I did hurt you in some way, emotionally or even spiritually, please forgive me too. I believe we are together in this learning process. And I highly hope for and appreciate any form of comments, and I think you already know of the many ways that we can get in touch. My email and website are available to you.

Coming back to the big question: do we need a Religiophilosophy Clinic? My answer is definitely Yes, with emphasis on the capital Y.

How about you?

Selected Bibliography

Al-Ghazali, A. H. M. (1997). *Al-Ghazali on disciplining the soul & breaking the two desires (Kitab riyadat al-nafs & kitab kasr al-shahwatayn) Books 22 and 23 of the revival of the religious sciences (Ihya ulum al-din)* (Winter, T.J., Trans.). Cambridge: Islamic Texts Society.

Al-Ghazali, A.H.M. (2011). *Revival of religion's sciences (Ihya' ulum ad-din)* (M.M. al-Sharif, Trans.). Beirut: Dar Al-Kotob Al-Ilmiyah.

Aristotle. (1999). *The metaphysics.* London, UK: Penguin Books Ltd.

Avicenna. (2005). *The metaphysics of the healing.* Utah: Foundation for Ancient Research and Mormon Studies (FARMS).

Black, A. (2001). *The history of Islamic political thought: From the prophet to the present.* New York, NY: Routledge.

Burns, E. (2018). *What is this thing called Philosophy of Religion?*

Oxon, OX and New York, NY: Routledge.

Covey, S. (2004). *The 7 habits of highly effective people*. New York, NY: Simon & Schuster.

Critchley, S. (2001). *Continental philosophy: A very short introduction*. Oxford, UK: Oxford University Press.

Darwin, C. (2004). *The origin of species*. New Zealand, NZ: Castle Publishing.

Descartes, R. (2005). *Discourse of method and the meditations*. United Kingdom, UK: Penguin Books Ltd.

Fakhry, M. (2004). *A history of Islamic philosophy*. New York, NY: Columbia University Press.

Hannam, J. (2009). *God's philosophers: How the Medieval world laid the foundations of modern science*. Icon Books Ltd.

Hawking, S. (1998). *A brief history of time*. New York, NY: Bantam Books.

Hick, J. (2007). *Evil and the God of love*. London, UK: Palgrave Macmillan.

Ian Shapiro (2012). *Moral Foundation of Politic*. United States, Yale University Press.

Ibn Qudāmah, Muwaffaq al-Dīn 'Abd Allāh ibn Aḥmad (1985). *Ibn Qudāma's Censure of Speculative Theology* (G. Makdisi, Trans.). London : E.J.W. Gibb Memorial Trust.

Inglehart, R. F. (2021). *Religion's sudden decline: What's causing it, and what comes next?* New York, NY: Oxford University Press.

Jensen, J. S. (2020). *What is religion?* New York, NY: Routledge.

Kaku, M. (2021). *The God equation: The quest for a theory of everything.* London, United Kingdom: Penguin Books Ltd.

Kant, I. (2020). *Groundwork of the metaphysics of morals.* Oxford: Oxford University Press.

Lang, J. (2004). *Losing my religion: A call for help.* Beltsville, MD: Amana Publications.

Leaman, O. (2009). *Islamic philosophy: An introduction.* United Kingdom, UK: Oxford.

Leibniz, G.W. (2008). *Theodicy.* Glos, GL: Echo-Library.com.

Lombard, M. (2009). *The golden age of Islam.* Princeton, NJ: Markus Wiener Publishers.

MacIntyre, A. (2007). *After virtue: A study in moral theory.* Notre Dame, Indiana: University of Notre Dame Press.

Manson, N. A. (2021). *This is philosophy of religion.* Hoboken, NJ: John Wiley & Sons, Inc.

Morgan, D. (2001). *The best guide to Eastern philosophy and religion.* New York, NY: Renaissance Media Inc.

Nadler, S. (2011). *Occasionalism: Causation among the cartesians.* New York, NY: Oxford University Press.

Nasr, S. H. (2006). *Islamic philosophy from its origin to the present: Philosophy in the land of prophecy.* New York, NY: State University of New York.

Numbers, R. L. (2006). *The creationists: From scientific creationism to intelligent design.* California: University of California Press.

Osho. (1994). *Osho Zen tarot: The transcendental game of Zen.* Italy: Osho International Foundation.

Paley, W. & Ware, J. (2012). *Natural theology or evidences of the existence and attributes of the deity.* Greenwood, WI: Suzeteo Enterprises.

Sandel, Michael J. (2010). *Justice: What's the right thing to do?* New York, NY: Farrar, Straus and Giroux.

Sartre, J.P. (2007). *Existentialism and humanism.* London, UK: Methuen Publishing Ltd.

Spencer, N. (2014). *Atheists: The origin of the species.* London: Bloomsbury Publishing Plc.

Taylor, C. (2007). *A secular age.* Massachusetts: The Belknap Press of Harvard University Press.

Tumin, M. (2019). *Asas teologi dan falsafah politik Muslim.* Kuala Lumpur, KL: University of Malaya Press.

Tumin, M. (2021). *Falsafah politik Barat masa kini: Metafizik dan tokoh.* Kuala Lumpur, KL: University of Malaya Press.

Vermes, G. (1981). *Jesus the Jew: A historian's reading of the Gospel*. Philadelphia: Fortress Press.

Weber, M. (2001). *The protestant ethic and the spirit of capitalism*. London: Routledge.

Winter, T. J. & Williams J.A. (2002). *Understanding Islam and the Muslims : The Muslim family and Islam and world peace*. Kentucky: Fons Vitae, US.